GOD IS...

PASTOR LERONE DINNALL

ISBN 978-1-956001-45-7 (hardcover)
ISBN 978-1-956001-46-4 (eBook)

Copyright © 2021 by Pastor Lerone Dinnall

All rights reserved. No part of this publication may be reproduced, distributed, or transmitted in any form or by any means, including photocopying, recording, or other electronic or mechanical methods without the prior written permission of the publisher.

Printed in the United States of America

"The Divine Spirit of God Invites all who will read this Book, that their minds will be set free to receive of The Manner that only God Alone can Give; God Bless you in The Almighty Name of Jesus Christ, Amen!"

Contents

TRIBUTES 1
INTRODUCTION 3
OPENING SCRIPTURE 6
MINDSET 8
THE ALTAR! 11
GOD IS… 19
GOD IS GOD 21
GOD IS CREATOR 35
GOD IS ABLE 39
GOD IS LOVE 44
GOD IS A DICTATOR..49
GOD IS FORGIVING 52
GOD IS TIMELY 56
GOD IS GOOD 61
GOD IS ALWAYS PRESENT 65
GOD IS JUSTIFIED 71
GOD IS MERCIFUL 75

GOD IS WORTHY	80
GOD IS THE BEST CHESS PLAYER	84
GOD IS NO RESPECTER OF PERSONS	87
GOD IS JEALOUS	89
GOD IS PATIENT	91
GOD IS IN ALL NATIONS, CULTURES AND TONGUES	95
GOD IS THE UNKNOWN	100
GOD IS IN IT	103
GOD IS NOT IN IT	108
GOD IS BALANCE	110
GOD'S SPIRITUAL LAWS	113
MISSING SPIRITUAL STEPS!	134
TOMORROW…	141
CLOSING SCRIPTURE	152
CONCLUSION	155

Tributes

"I Offer this Tribute to A Special Sister that is a member of The Church of Jesus Christ Fellowship Family, to Sister Tanya Fearon, she was the first person I gave this Message to, and after she read what The Message was saying unto her Soul, she said Pastor, this Message must be a Book by itself, separated from everything else because this Message will touch a lot of people's life. I can say to Sister Fearon that I've observed what The Lord has done in your life through these inspired words therefore I know through experience that if the word reaches a lot more souls, then a lot more people will be changed for the Glory of God's Kingdom. Thank you Sister Tanya Fearon for Inspiring me to Release this book to be a Message within a Manual for all people to know Who GOD IS. God's Richest Blessings".

"To All God's True Worshippers, The Lively Stones that keeps The Sacrifice Clean, that Allows God's Continual Favors to be Granted upon this corrupt Earth; May The Blessings of God Forever Be Released upon all that your hands will touch, May The Presence of God

Go before every Journey that you will take, May The Mark of God Be Sealed upon your foreheads and in your hands, In The Name Jesus Christ so let it be".

Introduction

All Glory Be Delivered unto The One God that Is Omnipotent, Omniscient and Omnipresent, To Jesus Christ The Lamb of God. It is a Wonderful Privilege for me The Servant of God to again Present to The World another Book from The Ministry of The Church of Jesus Christ Fellowship Savannah Cross, Jamaica, West Indies. This Book Entitled "GOD IS" is Book number four, and it is geared towards bringing all God's People from the Four Direction of The Earth into One Agreement and Language to Identify and to Acknowledge that there is Only One True and Living God which Manifest Himself in The Vessel of Jesus Christ.

Has it was identified in the beginning of The Book of The Gospel of St Matthew, the writer sought to manifest The Genealogy of Jesus Christ to thus establish undeniable proof that Jesus Christ Came from the lineage of David to correspond with the Prophecies that was laid out in The Manuscript by both Major Prophets and Minor Prophets. So it is that The Lord Has Identified the clear need for His People in this Time and Age to become fully knowledgeable of The Doctrine to Identify God In One.

This Book is Designed with the intention that the Readers can personalize their copy of this Book, by carrying this Book wherever they may go to replicate the custom that The Children of Israel Studied and Maintain for generations to wear frontlets upon their foreheads and also teach their children to do the same to thus maintain the Relationship to manifest at all times Who Their God Is to them. I'm confident that all People, Nations and Dominions that have received a copy of this Book, if these words are Studied to Identify that these words indeed does Manifest The Living God; if the disciplines to Maintain and Teach God Being One is Observed, then the same success that The Children of Israel benefited from The Living God will again be set as a Covenant of Peace for those who will walk in The Anointing of The One God Ministry.

GOD IS, this Book is geared towards answering a lot of Questions that were often time swept under the carpet because that which was asked, the intelligence was not given to answer that question, therefore leaving an unsatisfied gap within the lives of those who have asked technical questions in regards to The Manifestation of The GodHead. It is The Confidence of The Spirit of God within me that Burns with Great Approval to write this Manuscript that will also Burn The Approval of God in the lives of those who will read this Book.

GOD IS…

There is not much left to say about this Book in the Introduction, I would desire for my Readers to have The Spiritual Hunger of needing to read this Book to thus be Satisfied of the Answers that was Revealed by God in regards to Who He Is.

The Eternal Spirit of God Has Already Granted The Approval for this Book to be Written and then to be Published, therefore I'm satisfied that God's People will be Blessed by these words. All Glory, Honor and Praise Be Offered to The Unlimited Mind of The Universe, Jesus Christ The Lamb of God, Amen.

Opening Scripture

1 Timothy Chapter 3:16.

"And without controversy great is The Mystery of Godliness: God Was Manifested in the Flesh, Justified in the Spirit, Seen of Angels, Preached unto the Gentiles, Believed on in the World, Received up into Glory".

1 John Chapter 1.

"That which was from The Beginning, which we have heard, which we have seen with our eyes, which we have looked upon, and our hands have handled, of The Word of Life; For The Life was Manifested, and we have seen it, and bear witness, and shew unto you that Eternal Life, which was with The Father, and was Manifested unto us; That which we have seen and heard declare we unto you, that ye also may have Fellowship with us: and truly our Fellowship is with The Father, and with His Son Jesus Christ. And these things write we unto you, that your joy may be full. This then is the Message which we have heard of Him, and declare unto you, that God Is Light, and in Him is no darkness at all. If we say that we have Fellowship with Him, and walk in darkness, we lie, and do not the Truth: But if we walk in The Light, as He is in The Light, we have Fellowship one with another, and The Blood of Jesus Christ His Son Cleanseth us from all sin. If we say that we have no sin, we deceive ourselves, and The Truth is not in us. If we confess our sins, He Is Faithful and Just to Forgive us our sins, and to cleanse us from all unrighteousness. If we say that we have not sinned, we make Him A Liar, and His Word is not in us".

Mindset

- God Can Be Identified in Everything and in Everyone, all Nations, Cultures, and Languages.
- There is in Fact a True Manifestation of Who God Is in All Religions, even A TENTH.
- Every person has a Purpose to fulfill in The Ministry and Manifestation of God's Will Being Done.
- Whenever we have been born in The Full Manifestation to know Who God Is to the measurement that we are Permitted to know God, then that Knowledge is never to be kept to ourselves, but to be a Tool that will be used to Train others to be Born into that same Revelation that we have Received from God. We are only Given the Knowledge to make certain that we pass on the Knowledge to the generation which is to come.
- Having The Knowledge of Who God Is will also enable us to become Wise to a touch of what the devil's devices are, therefore allowing

us to become Spiritually Alert at all times of the Environment's Movement.
- God Is Eternal, therefore The Spirit of God in us has Access to Eternal Benefits.
- Every person we meet let us try our best to discover where in their life is The Manifestation of Who God Is, because it is there.
- At least 10% of the Attributes of a man resembles The Living God, our job is to generate that 10% to grow thus manifesting 100% of The Temple that God Needs for us to Become for His Will and His Glory Being Fulfilled.
- There is no man that ever lived, that is living now, and will live after us, that is not in need of The Special Ingredient of God's Touch to enable that man to become God's Tool, thus having God's Peace.
- Every Person, Nations, Languages and Dominions that have been Born in The Understanding to Know Who God Is, is indeed A Powerful Chosen People of which God Has Become their Defense. Anyone that fights God's People, it will be Revealed that they are fighting with God. God Never lost a Battle, it wasn't seen in the Past, it will not happen in the Present and the Future is as Solid as a Rock, because God Is The Eternal Rock.

- No One can disagree with A God That Is Eternal, because when we are gone because time is fulfilled, God Still Lives, thus His Purpose Will Still Be Established, If not by us who are now living, then by those who will live after us.

The Altar!

Message # 149   **Date Started August 5, 2020**
                      Date Finalized August 5, 2020.

Greetings Royal Family of God, I Present to you another wonderful Message, it will be good to identify the Knowledge that will spring from these words, not only for ourselves but also for our children to know. I'm happy to again be in this position of Grace and Favors to fulfill the destined purpose from The Hands of God. I will always point my readers to The True Source of Inspiration, that being our Lord and Saviour Jesus Christ, to Him Be All Glory, Honor and Praise Forever to Eternity, Amen.

    The True Strength of a man is never found in himself or in an item but rather, the true strength that a man can find to rely on always is the strength that has No Beginning and No Ending. This Strength is always Manifesting in The Invisible God. Early in Ministry when I just became a Minister I knew that God was in me but I never really knew who God Was; this started a burning of my desire to find out for myself who exactly is

God. Upon going through The Names of God from the beginning of The Bible to the end, and also identifying other Name for God in other books such as the Name Elohim, My Spirit was rather fixed on One Name of God that I never really got the full understanding of what it really means until The Lord Explained it to me; all the other Names of God are understandable, but when The Lord Asked me if I Knew what it means for Him to be called The Almighty God, I hesitated, because I Needed to know that I understood what it meant. It sounds basically straight forward to explain because it already reveals the meaning. The Lord then Told me to Ask Him what The Name Almighty God means. I asked The Lord what it means and this is what The Lord Explained:

"To Be The Almighty God, it means that if there could be a gathering of all the strengths and the powers and the governance and all the kingdoms throughout all dispensations from beginning to the end, from Spiritual to Physical and back again to Spiritual, and even if all those Powers, Strengths, Governance, Rules, Kingdoms and Dominions was to somehow joined together throughout all dispensations and stand as one, The Lord Said even if this was possible it could still not stand before Him because He Has All Might and All Strength, All Power and All Rule from Spiritual to Physical and then back to Spiritual"!

Now that we have an idea of what it truly means for God to Be Sovereign we can move on. The Altar: Truth, Man has always throughout all dispensation needed The Help of God to fashion their existence and also to secure the future Inheritance for their children to follow. Happy is the Man that knows this to be a Fact! There are many in this world that I've discovered for myself that are only interested in working for the day, there is no consideration in them to identify that all the work of a man must be carefully analyzed by that same man to make certain that the work is set for a Continual Blessing and not just a Now Blessing. But this knowledge is likened to foolishness to those who are not set for God's Divine Blessing. And because a man has to Now be Born in the understanding to gain the knowledge and wisdom of tomorrow, this man will find himself digging into Spirituality to find The Source of All Strength because that man is already knowledgeable that his strength is no strength if it cannot forcefully dictate that which will take place for the next evolution of himself.

A man needing the help of God always signifies a Personal Relationship with God, and with seeking to have a Personal Relationship with God, a man will find out through Seeking God's Face that there is none to be compared to God thus whatever that man is now doing to entreat God's Presence, that man will find out for himself that God's Presence can only be satisfied to remain at a Location that this man have made certain that such a

Location is not only special to himself but that Location now becomes special for The Presence of The Lord. This Location is first for a man's own vessel, and with knowing for yourself what it really takes to maintain your own vessel for The Glory of God's Presence, a man will now seek for wherever he now travels to manifest that same Presence of God within him to any Location he is now a part of. Keeping The Presence of God in our temple is the number one duty for a man of Destiny, because if the temple cannot be maintained with The Presence of God then wherever else that man will seek to manifest as an Altar for God will never be able to sustain God's Presence because the Foundation vessel is no longer in agreement with God's Presence for His Presence to Remain within that temple.

A Man Growing with The Presence of The Lord will now seek for the likeness of the same Presence from God that is within Him to now move anywhere else that he now travels. A Man will find The Likeness of The Presence of God within a Church, and because of this a man will grow to love that Church and build that Church and Maintain that Church all because of The Likeness of The Same Presence of God that is within himself is also found within The Assembly of that Church. A Man will seek and will find the likeness of The Presence of The Lord within a woman, and a man will Love that woman because of the Same Likeness of God's Presence that is found within her, a man will then build a life with this woman, he will have children with this woman, he will maintain this woman throughout life's struggles all because of the Sure Manifestation of God's Divine Presence that is also found within this woman. A Man will have friends based on the Likeness of God's Presence that is manifesting within these people, a man will feel comfortable to talk with these new friends because of God's Presence within them, around them and around everyone that they have company with. A man will identify within himself that the more he finds People, Places and Things with the Likeness of the same Manifestation that he has developed with His God, he will identify that the same Altar for God that is within himself is built to a greater Anointing which will reveal that this man will be able to receive Greater Favors from God based on the Greater Presence of The Holy God that is manifesting within him and around his entire circle.

Those are the good parts of a Man's Altar to God, and using the term **"MAN"** in this message clearly means mankind. Let's get to the dangerous side of a Man's Altar. A Man that has established an Altar for God must also identify that he has also established an Altar for himself that his whole Might, Body and Soul is directly linked to that Altar that is now Established. Therefore it is very important for that man to make certain that he is always aware of what is taking place for that which he has established to be an Altar for God and with God. Because a man is directly linked to his Altar, if the Altar is Building towards Spiritual Growth then that man will also Spiritually Grow in God. If The Altar has now become corrupt through the direction of People, Places and Things, then that man because he is of that Altar and Spiritually linked to that Altar, that man will become also corrupt if that man have not now decided to cut all Relationship that is now in constant agreement with that same Altar. And if not cutting the Relationship, then that man must make certain that his Altar returns to a state of cleansing that will reveal repentance and maintain again the full Standard of what the Altar is meant to Fulfill.

There is only One True Altar which is The Direct Link from that Man's vessel to God. A man branches from that Main Altar to now establish Continued Altar of The Same Manifestation and Likeness of God's Presence. Therefore a man must be quick to identify whenever a Continued Altar is now become corrupt, because if the Altar Relationship that was developed with The Church, Wife and Friends is now different from The Likeness it was first manifested to be of God's Presence, then that same difference in the Altar of the Church, Wife and Friends will now spread immediately to the Main and Sure Altar that was first Established with The Temple.

A Man has to be watchful of what takes place within and upon their Altar. If a Lie is being Manifested upon and within a Man's Altar it therefore means that a Lie will never leave and continue to grow for the complete life span of that Man's Altar; and if a Lie is Fixed in that Man's Altar it therefore means that God's Presence is no longer The Strength for that Man's Altar. An Altar is also a Direct Covenant with God as to what the Relationship will be like for that man and their God. If any changes are made for the Direct Rule of what The Purpose of The Altar should be, then it will automatically result in a breaking of The Covenant that was Fixed for The Relationship of that Altar. A man must always seek to maintain the standards of his Altar because if The Covenant is broken then God's Almighty Strength is lifted from the life of that man. Therefore, no more coverage from the enemy, no more deliverance, no more victory, no more Glory of God's Presence with you in whatever environment you may travel to, also, no more extended Altar manifestation, The Spiritual Walls are completely torn down. Then it will be identified by that man that their Altar was never A Church, it was never their Wife, it was never found within their Friends, but The True Altar was always found within a person's temple. How Sure is our temple for God's Use, this will manifest the Ultimate Strength of our Altar with God!

Genesis Chapter 35:1-7.

"And God Said unto Jacob, Arise, Go up to Bethel, and dwell there: and make there an Altar unto God, that appeared unto thee when thou fleddest from the face of Esau thy brother. Then Jacob said unto his household, and to all that were with him, Put away

the strange gods that are among you, and be clean, and change your garments: And let us arise, and go up to Bethel; and I will make there an Altar unto God, who answered me in the day of my distress, and was with me in the way which I went. And they gave unto Jacob all the strange gods which were in their hand, and all their earrings which were in their ears; and Jacob hid them under the oak which was by Shechem. And they Journeyed: and the Terror of God was upon the cities that were round about them, and they did not pursue after the sons of Jacob. So Jacob came to Luz, which is in the land of Canaan, that is, Bethel, he and all the people that were with him. And he Built there an Altar, and called the place Elbethel: Because there God Appeared unto him, when he fled from the face of his brother".

Again I say, All Glory, Honor and Praise be directed to The Only Living God, Jesus Christ Forever to Eternity, Amen. From Pastor Lerone Dinnall and The Ministry of The Church of Jesus Christ Fellowship, Savannah Cross, Jamaica, West Indies. God's Favors Continually.

"Is My Altar Connected To The Eternal Source Of All Strength"?

_____.

GOD IS…

Message # 101   Date Started November 13, 2018.
                 Date Finalized December 12, 2018.

Let Us Begin With Prayer...

"Father of Heaven and Earth, I come before Your Presence this Night asking for Your Divine Approval in The Matchless Name of Jesus Christ, that Your Servant will be able to write for Your Glory, and that Your Reflection can be Seen through everything that my hands will write to be of Inspiration to all those who will Read of this Divine Message, which will no doubt act has a Tour guide for all those who have not yet been Born of the Belief and Anointing to know of a surety that The God of The Universe Indeed Does Fill the very Atmosphere. Lord I Pray for Divine Intelligence, that Your People will be Fed from The Heavenly Manner, which only Your Voice can Speak. Father of Heaven and Earth, I Pray that You Will Allow for this Message to Stand has A Pillar of

Righteousness, and A Pillar of Strength for all Times, that Your People will forever be Able to read this Message for Divine Inspiration to Move Directly into what You Have Destined for their lives and will move without Doubt to know that God Who Is Our Father Is The God of The Impossible. I ask for Your Divine Approval Only in The Name of Jesus Christ, Amen".

To God Be All The Glory Great Things He Has Done. I am Privileged to be in this Position, that I'm again found worthy to be God's Instrument to write A Message that will no Doubt be of Divine Inspiration to God's People. Being Touched By The Hands of God on this Night being the 13th of November 2018 around the time of 11:30 pm. God Produced A Burning that Removed sleep, seeing that I've not received a full night's sleep for two days now, and this night I decided that I was going to make up for those lost times of sleep, by retiring to bed early on November 13, 2018. Now I know what Jeremiah was speaking about, when he said I feel like Fire shut up in my bones. On this night The Lord Gave Me this Topic and Said Get up and Begin to Write about A Topic Called GOD IS. Let's get to it.

CHAPTER 1

GOD IS GOD

Exodus Chapter 19:16-19.

"And it came to pass on the third day in the morning, that there were thunders and lightnings, and a thick cloud upon the mount, and the Voice of the trumpet exceeding loud; so that all the people that was in the camp trembled. And Moses brought forth the people out of the camp to meet with God; and they stood at nether part of the mount. And mount Sinai was altogether on a smoke, because The Lord Descended upon it in fire: and the smoke thereof ascended as the smoke of a furnace, and the whole mount quaked greatly. And when The Voice of the Trumpet sounded long, and waxed louder and louder, Moses spake, and God Answered him by A Voice".

Exodus Chapter 20:18-21.

"And all the people saw the Thunderings, and the Lightnings, and the noise of the Trumpet, and the mountain smoking: and when the people saw it, they removed, and stood afar off. And they said unto Moses, Speak thou with us, and we will hear: but let not God Speak with us, lest we die. And Moses said unto the people, Fear not: for God Is Come to Prove you, and that His Fear may be before your faces, that ye sin not. And the people stood afar off, and Moses drew near unto the thick darkness where God Was".

Have we ever noticed that for many that speak about God, it would be compared that God is just another thing or object that you use at this moment and the next moment you decide to cast it aside like He is replaceable. Having not yet come to the Understanding of Who God Is, will prove to be Destructive to all People, Nations, and Tongues.

I was recently challenged regarding one of my Messages that The Lord Allowed for me to write; that Message is Called The Lord Visits. The Query was by A Minister of Religion. And he wanted to let me know that regarding what I wrote about The Lord Visiting the Land was a Statement that did not make any sense because God Is Always upon the Land. Now let us use this Message to

Identify the Depths and Heights of God, because many are still not Understanding Who God Is.

To a level looking at what the Minister said to me regarding God Always being on the land is understandable; but to suggest that the Message does not make sense, is entering into territory that you're now denouncing what God Has Revealed. I would say to any person that questioned what these Messages Reveal, good luck with that mind frame. Because everything that God Has Revealed will one day Bring forth a Manifestation, and those who took the Warning would have Positioned themselves to ensure that they are in The Will of God, thus proving that they are under The Protection of God for that day which is to come.

Writing Messages is not something I picked up, I never even wrote before being A Pastor, and I never did it as an Option in School; Therefore, This is A Talent that The God Of The Universe Has Revealed through my Vessel. I'm Asked to write rather than having the desire to write. I'm Burned with Hunger to write for God while I'm in my Bed sleeping at nights and in the Early Morning of sleep when every other person is sleeping. While I'm asleep, and I immediately awoke from sleep, my wife knows what has happened, and also knows that I will be spending the early morning writing Inspired Messages for God. Writing for God Has Now Become A Joy for my life, to Know that God Created A Special

Purpose for my Life to reach His People. To God Be The Glory, Great Things He Has Done.

But let us have a Look at The Mind Of God. Has I responded to that Minister, to ask the Question if he actually thinks that God Is Always Walking on the land.

God In His Ultimate Form and Glory, The Earth Cannot Contain Him, The Earth Cannot even Stand before The Full Presence of The God of The Universe. Man in Sinful Flesh Cannot go before The Eternal Fire that Cannot Be Quenched. The Bible mentions that it took God's Righteousness to make us Righteous before God, to allow for us to understand that without God's Assistance, there was nothing we could have done by ourselves or through Sacrifice that could have sanctified us unto Righteousness. There was no amount of Burnt of Offering and Sacrifice throughout generations that could have Satisfied the hunger of the Perfect Sacrifice that is made to cover mankind to again be in The Presence of God. When Adam and Eve Sinned, God Had to Remove them from The Spiritual Realm because they could no longer be in The Presence of God. Everything and Everyone is considered to be Unworthy to Stand Before and In The Full Presence and Manifestation of The Almighty God.

Revelations Chapter 1:9-19.

"I John, who also am your brother, and companion in tribulation, and in the kingdom and patience of

Jesus Christ, was in the isle that is called Patmos, for The Word of God, and for The Testimony of Jesus Christ. I was in The Spirit on The Lord's Day, and heard behind me a great voice, as of a trumpet, Saying, I Am Alpha and Omega, The First and The Last: and, What thou seest, write in a Book, and send it unto the seven churches which are in Asia; unto Ephesus, and unto Smyrna, and unto Pergamos, and unto Thyatira, and unto Sardis, and unto Philadelphia, and unto Loadicea. And I turned to see The Voice that Spake with me. And being turned, I saw seven golden candlesticks; And in the midst of the seven candle sticks One Like unto The Son of Man, clothed with a garment down to The Foot, and girt about the paps with a golden girdle. His Head and His Hairs Were White like wool, as white as snow; and His Eyes were as A Flame of Fire; And His Feet like unto Fine Brass, as if they burned in a furnace; and His Voice as the sound of Many Waters. And He Had in His Right Hand Seven Stars: and out of His Mouth Went A Sharpe Twoedged Sword: And His Countenance was as The Sun Shineth in His Strength. And when I saw Him, I fell at His Feet as dead. And He Laid His Right Hand upon me, Saying unto me, Fear Not; I Am The First and The Last: I Am He that Liveth, and was Dead; and, Behold, I Am Alive For Evermore, Amen; and Have The Keys of Hell and of

Death. Write the things which thou hast seen, and the things which are, and the things which shall be hereafter".

Revelation Chapter 6:12-17.

"And I beheld when he opened the sixth seal, and, lo, there was a Great Earthquake; and The Sun became Black as Sackcloth of hair, and the Moon became as Blood; And The Stars of Heaven Fell unto the Earth, even as a fig tree casteth her untimely figs, when she is shaken of a mighty wind. And The Heaven Departed as a Scroll when it is rolled together; and every mountain and Island were moved out of their places. And the kings of the earth, and the great men, and the rich men, and the chief captains, and the mighty men, and every bondman, and every free man, hid themselves in the dens and in the rocks of the mountains; And said to the mountains and rocks, Fall on us, and hide us from The Face of Him that Sitteth on The Throne, and from The Wrath of The Lamb: For The Great Day of His Wrath Is Come; and who shall be able to stand?"

Revelation Chapter 20:11.

"And I saw A Great White Throne, and Him that Sat on it, from whose Face

the Earth and Heaven Fled away; and there was found no place for them".

And this is where the confusion comes in for a lot of Christians that actually believe that there is more than One GOD. Because The Bible Said that God Sent Forth His Son to die for the sin of The World. The Revelation of God Revealed and it is a Fact that God Actually Prepared Himself to Die; but The Eternal Spirit of God Cannot Die, therefore, God Prepared A Vessel made of Flesh and Called the Vessel in which He Has Filled to be His Son, known as Jesus Christ, The Mediator between The Eternal Spirit of God and Mankind. Jesus Christ Is A Replica of what God Looks like for mankind to walk and talk, to handle and to experience what it is like to be in The Presence of God's Will Being Done. Because the Only Sacrifice that could have Redeemed Adam's Fallen Race was A Sacrifice of Perfection. And The Bible Said that The Heavens are not Clean in His Eyes, then where else could that Perfect Sacrifice come from?

_____.

If The Heavens is not Clean to God, that means the Inhabitants of The Heavens is also considered to be not Clean and Unworthy to offer that Sacrifice, and were not even considering Earth and the Inhabitant of Earth; because if Heaven is not clean, how can Earth be in the conversation.

The Perfect Plan of God Revealed that He Is The Perfect Sacrifice; but there still remains the Condition, that God Had to Come in The Physical in order for the Sacrifice to be Accepted. Even though the Sacrifice would have already been Done in The Spiritual, it needed also to be Fulfilled in The Physical. God Had to Walk with man and Teach mankind what is The Will and Pathway to Please God, this an attitude that mankind had lost from the Foundation of the Earth. Jesus Christ Was and Is The Full Manifestation of God In The Flesh, but He Was Limited to Be The Full Manifestation of God Almighty; thus always referring to The Eternal Spirit Has His Father. Because The Eternal God Is and Remains to Be Complete SPIRIT. Therefore, Jesus Christ Was A Full Measurement of God's Spirit within A Vessel, and that Measurement of God's Spirit within Jesus Christ was just A Faction of The Completion of Who God Is In Full Manifestation.

Therefore, Being in the Flesh He Could Not Stand Worthy to be Called God, because if He was that Full Manifestation, the Earth could not contain Him; but rather to a Lesser Authority to be Called The Son of God, Because of The Limitation of The Vessel that He Was In. Being Knowledgeable of The Complete Manifestation of God, there is no way even An Unspotted Lamb could be compared to Be God in Full Measure. Every Vessel of God carries the limitation of An Authority within that Vessel, thus we are always subject to The Greater Authority that can never be fully contained in any Vessel, and that Greater Authority and Anointing Is The Eternal Spirit and Fire of God that Cannot be Measured or Quenched. Every Child of God that is Present and was before us, and that will be after us, is Fixed with only Having Obtained and Receiving An Anointing that Resembles and Reflect that being of A Son of God. A Son of God Anointing and Authority Still Remains to be The Reflection of God's Character on Earth for His Will to be Established.

Therefore, A Son of God is still Dependent Upon The True Source from which his strength comes from. Thus we have the confusion of many that believe that there are three Gods, because it reads in The Bible that Jesus Christ at times went to Pray to His Father and was seen Praying to His Father. This was done to show Proof that even though God Was In The Flesh, that Body being The Manifestation of Jesus Christ was Still Limited because He Could Not Rely on His own Abilities and Gifts which were in Measurement, Meaning Portions; thus The Unlimited Infinite Eternal Spirit of God that Sits on His Throne was referred to as Father when it was that Jesus Christ Prayed.

We that are Saved Can Identify for ourselves this Fact: Before We Received The Gift of The Holy Ghost with all The Benefits and Fruits of The Spirit; Whose Gift was it?

_____.

And The Spirit of God Having Found A Dwelling Place to Manifest God's Will; Who Remains Being The Source?_____.

Is it not God?_____.

Therefore, If we Testify that we Operate only through The Manifestation of The Spirit of God, does that make us to be God?_____.

Seeing that God's Will is Being Fulfilled in our Vessel, should we be called God?

_____.

Or should we take the Position that was laid out for us through The Example of Jesus Christ, to refer our actions that Pleases God, to thus call ourselves A Son of God.

What do you think?_____.

Are we considered to Be God because of a Portion of God's Gift, or is it that we are Under The Authority of Being A Son of God? We Are

_____.

Bringing forth a suitable Answer for the Query of the Minister and for those who are of the same Opinion, I will ask this Question: Is it God, The Eternal Spirit that Actually Visits the Land daily, or is it that God Has Sons of God and Messengers on the Earth in the form of Angels that Ascends and Descends to Manifest The Word of God, which is The Spirit of God, and to Bring Information to The God of The Universe?

What do you think?_____.

GOD IS...

Angels that Carries The Commands of God, are they not Fulfilling God's Purpose; Thus Establishing God's Spirit in all the Earth?_____.

Sons of God that Perform God's Duty, are they not spreading The Spirit of God within the Earth; Thus Manifesting God's Presence upon the land?_____.

Therefore, To a level I Understand that God's Spirit Is Always on The Land; but we've got to Elevate our thinking to Understand that The Almighty Presence and Eternal Fire of God Is Not Actually WALKING on The land each day, or else there will be no Earth for us to live on. The Children of Israel Begged Moses to Speak to God, because if God Continued to Speak to them DIRECTLY, they would have all Died. That's how Serious The Full Manifestation of God Is.

Then we wonder why it is that we come to Church, and there are many that sit inside The Church performing actions that should not be performed within The Church, and everyone and everything remains to be the same, no Fear of considering that they are in The Presence of God. The reason for this action of no fear for God's Presence in His House, is because there is no Presence of God Within That Church, or The Presence of God Within that Church is Weak. Not that God is weak; but rather The Temple in which God Should Have Full Control is Weak. And That's The Truth, The whole Truth and nothing but The Truth.

God Sends Forth His Word and it is Received and Fulfill Missions of God's Will Being Done On Earth as it is In Heaven. Therefore, I said to the Minister: That which is always with us is God's Spirit in the form of The Holy Ghost in us by measurement, and also God's Angel Bringing forth God's Messages, therefore, The Whole World is Filled with The Spirit of God to A Measurement based on God's Word. I let the Minister know that what I was referring to in The Message Called The Lord Visits, was not The Word of God in circulation by means of us who are Filled with The Holy Ghost or by Using His Messengers within the Form of being Angels, but rather, what I was referring to, is the Fact that God Said:

"His Eternal Presence to A Measurement Will Visit The Land".

This Presence of God in Measurement, Will See the things that are happening to thus Fulfill God's Will, and not man's will.

It is mentioned in The Book of Genesis Chapter 18:20-21.

"And The Lord Said, Because The Cry of Sodom and Gomorrah is Great, and because their sin is very grievous; I Will Go Down, and See whether they have done altogether according to The Cry of it, which is come unto Me; and if not, I Will Know".

GOD IS...

The Lord Said The Cry Came up before Him; this is letting us know that God Has been Receiving Information based on what is Happening, by means of those who are Serving The Living God through their Prayers, and by means of Angels that Ascend and Descend to Carry out their Duties that they are Assigned to Fulfill. And by these Servants Fulfilling that which is Required by God; This now Allows for God to Develop Intelligence, of which when the Vessel with The Cry of The Saints is Full, The Eternal Presence of God Moves with Intentions of Action, with the Desire to See for Himself, if what is Reported is Actually being Manifested. Can I say that wherever God's Eternal Spirit Visits, it did not end well for that place that The Lord Chooses to have A Look and to Walk.

The Lord Said I Will Go Down; This is allowing God's People to recognize that God's Eternal Spirit Will Only Come Down when it is that there is an Overwhelming of what is Happening on the land, to thus Move with Divine Force to Uproot those things and Altars which are not of His Will Being Done. Wherever in The Bible it is Mentioned that God Came Down, there was always a great altering of the Earth in that the very EarthQuakes at The Presence of God. In The Book of Exodus it Reveals that the Mountain was on Smoke and Quaked, because God's Eternal Presence Being Unquenched Fire was upon the Mountain.

Note: This Presence of God that was experienced by The Children of Israel was still in Measurement, and was not of The Full Glory that God Possess.

The Tower of Babel was being built and God Came Down to See for Himself what was being done, thus Discovering that what was being done was not in Accordance with God's Will for The Earth. Therefore, God Confused the Language of those who were Building that Tower and Scattered the people all over the World. Genesis Chapter 11:1-9.

CHAPTER 2

GOD IS CREATOR

Genesis Chapter 1:1-3.

"In the beginning God Created The Heaven and The Earth. And The earth was without form, and void; and darkness was upon the face of the deep. And The Spirit of God Moved upon the face of the waters. And God Said, Let There Be Light: And there was Light".

St John Chapter 1:1-5.

"In the Beginning was The Word, and The Word Was With God, and The Word Was God. The same was in the beginning With God. All things were Made by Him; and without Him was not anything Made that was Made. In Him was life; and the life

was the light of men. And The Light Shineth in darkness; and the darkness comprehended it not".

Being Creator, there is absolutely nothing that creation would have become that God Is Not Fully Aware of what is the Potential for His Creation to become and now Is. Does this Surprise or Stop God from Doing and Fulfilling the Destiny of that which is to be fulfilled in the lives of those who Trust in The Living God?

_____.

The Answer is No!

It is well Documented in The Bible Speaking about God Being The Creator of Everything In The Beginning. Now that everything is already Created; does this Action of Creation Being Made, does it Stop God or Limits The Unlimited Mind of The Universe from that Divine Order of still Being The Creator?

_____.

The Answer is No!

There are Levels of Spirituality that A Child of God must climb in order to recognize God to Be What He Says He Is. And God Will Stress on a particular point in A Child of God life to Establish that which He Already Is, but we have not yet known God to Be of that Revelation,

GOD IS...

because we have not been Seasoned or Shaped to that type of Relationship with God. When The Lord Appeared to Moses in A Burning Bush which was not Consumed, this event caused Moses to have a look for himself, because this was in fact something that no one could identify has being normal; and God Needed for Moses to be Born in The Revelation to Know that he was now in The Presence of The Impossible God. That encounter with God Is A Rebirth of the physical mind to now Transform to be of The Spiritual Mind to Know that GOD IS…..

_____.

Every Revelation of God to His People is an Experience that Remains with that Servant, and nothing can change you after you have Personally Experience God's Presence for yourself.

As it is Revealed in The Scripture, God Said to Moses, I AM THAT I AM. Bringing forth the full Manifestation to know that before we came into contact to know about God, He Was Already God, and has been Reigning as God before Time Came into Existence. It also Brings to our Understanding to know that at the time in our lives that we came to discover that there is A God; this Revelation is only new to us, because God Is Already Fully Set to Demonstrate in whatever time period, whether it is the Past, Present or the Future of people being Born in The Revelation that God Will Continue To Be GOD.

It doesn't matter how far Creation Moves away from its intended Purpose and Position; and it doesn't matter how far gone a person may think that their life is gone from God. Being Creator and Main Architect, God Is Aware of what it Will Take to Manifest again that which will be for His Glory and His Purpose. But the Main thing we need to Understand is that God Moves to Manifest His Purpose and His Glory. Therefore, If The Creator Is Going to Step Into the Lives of His People, it is a Sure Guarantee, that what is to be Fulfilled, will only be Manifested to allow those whose lives have been Changed, to Reflect A Sacrifice to Give Continual Glory to The King of kings and The Lord of lords; because God's Will Must Be Done.

CHAPTER 3

GOD IS ABLE

There are times that will present itself in our lives, that we have completely lost all confidence in our own Abilities, and it would seem that we have lost all confidence in that which we desire for our Father to Fulfill. Because it would have been experienced in our Lives that God Has Forgotten about His Children. There are Seasons that God Has Placed within His Power and Time, that is doesn't matter how Long and Hard We Cry, if The Seasons for that which is to be Fulfilled within God's Time is not Ripe, then that which we would have Desired from God to Fulfill will not be Experienced. There is one Clear Fact for God's People to Understand:

"God Moves To Fulfill His Glory!"

A Child of God Has to be Born of The Spirit of Patience, to therefore Rest in God and know Fully that God Will Perform Everything for His Children for the Benefit of His Will and Glory Being Fulfilled. This means that when God Has Fulfilled that which was Impossible to A Servant of God, all that will remain within the life of that Servant is A Spirit of Gratitude for all times for The Service of God.

Genesis Chapter 18:14.

"Is anything too hard for The Lord? At the time appointed I Will Return unto thee, according to the time of life, and Sarah Shall Have A Son".

That which should be reflecting in our minds is the words that Declare and Decree:

"Is anything too hard for The Lord"?
_____.

The next focus must be the words:

"At the time Appointed I Will Return unto thee".

Relationship with God Must Be Maintained if that which is Promised should reach the Accepted time of Harvest. There will arise many Temptations for a person that is Waiting on God's Time, to break the contract of their Deliverance, because they've now become Frustrated, accepting the devil's trick to believe that God Is Not Able.

I Will Give My Testimony for The Benefit of this Topic, to Reveal to My Readers that Nothing can stop God's Purpose within the life of those who are Destined for Service.

Being of the age of 10 to 12 years old, I remember being told everywhere I went, that I was not going to become anything in this life. If I went to School, this Message was the subject for my School; if I'm on the road, it was a Doctrine. I could not go anywhere and was not reminded of what the devil was using people to tell me of what I would become. I'm a strong believer after this experience that a person's Environment Dictates their Behavior and Future. After a while, that which was being Preached to me by the devil's worker, now became a firm belief within my own life. I started to believe everything that people told me I would become. I remember one day when I came from School, the recording of my Future began to play; I remember being Frustrated, I went in my house and took a knife and decided that if I'm not Destined to become something in life, I might as well end my own life.

Becoming a Pastor made me realize that this past experience allowed me to identify those who are plagued with the same spirits of frustration, to force that person of wanting to put an end to that which they are experiencing. I was able through The Discernment of The Holy Ghost to meet three persons at different times, that was plagued with this same spirit of suicide, to turn from that which they were intended to fulfill upon their lives. I'm also of the belief that if I share this Testimony in this Message, I believe my Testimony will be able to save a lot more than three people. This Testimony will be Able to save Thousands of people for The Glory of God's Kingdom.

Let's get back to the Testimony; I took the knife and went to a place which was my secret hideout, when I decided to place the knife at my chest and started to press; I Heard A Voice, not really sure of where The Voice was coming from, but I knew of a certainty that there was A Voice. And The Voice Said:

"What Are You Doing?

**Do You Not See That It Is Painful To Die?
Put Away The Knife.
I Will Make You To Become Something
For Me In Life".**

Being of the age of 10 or 12, I knew that I heard The Voice of God, because where I was, there was no one there. After that Voice Spoke, I returned home with Peace in my heart, no longer of any concern what people thought about me, because it doesn't matter; A Voice

Told me the opposite of what everyone else would seek to allow me to believe. I went home and gave the knife to my Grandmother and received a beating because I took the knife. After the beating I was still Fixed in what The Voice Told me. I had Peace.

Three people received this Testimony that I was afraid to utter because I was concerned about how people would now look at me. But having shared this Testimony with three persons that were taking the wrong road, I discovered that they believed in what I told them and their lives are now Changed for The Better and not for the Worst. Who could it be, no one else but The God Who Is Able. And this happened when I was between the age of 10 or 12. The Able God Knew What He Would Make me to Become, before I even knew what I would Become for God.

Today I'm A Pastor, Preaching and Teaching, Writing Messages to Inspire God's People all over The World, no wonder the devil tried so hard to cause me to kill myself. To God Be All The Glory, Great Things He Had Done.

I'm no longer ashamed of this Testimony; I've outgrown Shame and Fear. For those who will read this Message, be encouraged to know that each person can Fulfill The Will of God. And God Is Especially Looking for that person that believes that their life has no meaning. God Is Able to Fill your Life with Divine Meaning and Service for His Kingdom. Yes, Yes, Yes, I'm Filled with Purpose for God's Glory.

CHAPTER 4

GOD IS LOVE

St John Chapter 3:16.

"For God So Loved the world, that He Gave His only begotten Son, that whosoever believeth in Him should not perish, but have everlasting life".

1 John Chapter 3:1-2.

"Behold, what manner of love The Father hath Bestowed upon us, that we should be called the sons of God: Therefore the world knoweth us not, because it knew Him not. Beloved, now are we the sons of God, and it doth not yet appear what we shall be: but we know that, when He Shall Appear, we shall be like Him; for we shall see Him as He Is".

GOD IS...

1 John Chapter 4:7-13.

"Beloved, let us love one another: for love is of God; and every one that loveth is born of God, and knoweth God. He that loveth not knoweth not God; for God Is Love. In this was manifested the love of God toward us, because that God Sent His Only Begotten Son into the world, that we might live through Him. Herein is love, not that we loved God, but that He Loved us, and Sent His Son to be the propitiation for our sins. Beloved, if God So Loved us, we ought also to love one another. No man hath seen God at any time. If we love one another, God Dwelleth in us, and His Love is Perfected in us. Hereby know we that we dwell In Him, and He In us, because He Hath Given us of His Spirit".

I'm often Teaching The Church on this Topic of Love, to let us Understand that Love does not exist without the Word and Action called **Sacrifice**. Just as how there is no Faith without the evidence of work being done. There is more time spent ensuring that whatever is really Loved is Maintained Untouched for the Preserving of that which is Loved to fulfill Its Desired Purpose. A Physical man cannot and will never Understand what is Love; it Now Requires For A Spiritual Man Being Born of The Will and Purpose of God to Understand Exactly what is The Meaning of God's Love. Love is not a speech, it's not unfulfilled desires or those desires that are fulfilled with intentions towards another person, but rather, Love is an Action that Preserves the full purpose of those who are being Loved.

If it is that through love by another person, our True Manifestation of what we should become for God's Glory is Altered or Killed, then it means that those who Profess that they loved us, were in Fact lying to us; thus it is proven by the Manifestation of who we've become under the Influence of their love. This is the reason why so many that are not Born of The Spirit of God are Confused, because we are still identifying Love as A Feeling and not as A Purpose. Those who are Called and Chosen for God's Service, are those who are In line with The Words of God that Says:

"Let Thy Will Be Done".

Psalms 3:4.

"But know that The Lord hath Set Apart him that is godly for Himself: The Lord Will Hear when I call unto Him".

There is Found in the Seasons when God Is Setting Aside those who are godly, in this event, it would seem to be that God Is Intentionally Preventing His Chosen Believers from Certain Activities and Opportunities of this World; of which this Statement is True. Because of Love from Our Father, there are many Doors and Gates to Opportunities in this life that Will and Must Remain to be Closed, until The Father Have Identified that we have Acquired the Level of Anointing to Overcome the Negative Effects of Those Opportunities.

Because of Love, it is The Father's Plan to Ensure that Those Blessings and Opportunities that are Given to A Son of God, is Able within The Anointing of That Same Son of God to Remain for The Purpose and Benefit of That Child of God. It is identified that those in this life that have received a Blessing, and found that they cannot keep that Blessing; It is The Revelation from The Father Above that Declared to me, that such a person did not allowed for The Anointing of God to Grow within their Vessel, that would Manifest that they are now Able to Keep that which God Has Given. Another view that was Revealed to me was that which was not able to remain with A Son of God, is that which God Has Not Given to A Son of God. And we are living witnesses; there are many things in this life that we have Forced our way to Receive, rather than Asking God if that which is desired, is the same that would become of Benefit for the walk of A Child of God.

To Understand The Purpose of God to His Children, Is to Be Born of The Knowledge that God Is The Beginning, The Present and The Future; The Three Views of God, thus Manifesting All The Benefits that A

Son of God Must Receive through His Will Being Done in Our lives. But there Must Be Established in our lives The Spirit of Trust for God's Actions within our lives, to know that all Actions from God Indeed spell the words: LOVE FOR HIS CHILDREN.

CHAPTER 5

GOD IS A DICTATOR

Isaiah Chapter 40:12-17.

"Who hath Measured the waters in The Hollow of His Hand, and meted out Heaven with a span, and comprehended the dust of the Earth in a measure, and weighed the Mountains in scales, and the Hills in a balance? Who hath directed The Spirit of The Lord, or Being His counseller hath Taught Him? With whom took He Counsel, and who Instructed Him, and Taught Him Knowledge, and shewed to Him the way of Understanding? Behold, the Nations are as a drop of a bucket, and are counted as the small dust of the balance: Behold, He Taketh up the Isles as a very little thing. And Lebanon is not sufficient for a burnt offering. All

Nations before Him are as Nothing; and they are counted to Him less than nothing, and Vanity".

Isaiah Chapter 40:25-26.

"To Whom then will ye liken Me, or shall I Be equal? Saith The Holy One. Lift up your eyes on high, and behold Who Hath Created these things, that Bringeth out their host by number: He Calleth them all by names by The Greatness of His Might, for that He Is Strong in Power; not one Faileth".

St Matthew Chapter 6:10.

"Thy Kingdom come. Thy Will Be Done in Earth, as it is in Heaven".

We are often found in the Position that there is Born in us the belief that we can do what we want to do when we feel like doing what we want to do. This Mind set however brings forth a Default In The Constitutional Laws of God, that Forcefully Demonstrates that all things Fulfill God's Will and Move According to God's Divine Purpose.

There is The Divine Purpose of God to Establish His Kingdom; and there must also be the Understanding Born in us to be Knowledgeable, that there is also The Divine Purpose In God to Destroy the kingdom of

Darkness. Therefore, For those who believe that they can just do what they feel like doing when they intend to do. Have we not recognized that if a person's actions Manifest Good in God's Eye, and also, if a person's actions Manifest Evil in God's Eye; by The Spirit of Wisdom it is Identified that God's Will and Divine Purpose is Being Fulfilled.

The Judgement Day Is Already Set, and those who are to Inherit The Kingdom of God, have already Received of that Blessing. Therefore, every single person is already FIXED in their Divine Purpose that they Must walk in to Fulfill their Position before The Judgement Seat of God, to Inherit Eternal Damnation or to Fulfill their Purpose to Inherit Eternal Rest in The Kingdom of God. As it stands, we are not doing what we feel like doing, when we want to do those things, to thus Interrupt God's Plan, but rather, every actions that is Manifested by each Individual, this Manifestation of our Actions Positions us for God's Will and Divine Purpose.

CHAPTER 6

GOD IS FORGIVING

Fact: If there was no Action of Forgiveness, there would not be a Mankind. The first and most Important Ingredient to understand about Forgiveness is for us to become Knowledgeable that the person who is doing the Forgiveness would at first have to Love that which they are Offering Forgiveness to. If there was no Love, then Forgiveness cannot be realized, because there is no mind set to preserve that which a person who is being Forgiven can become in the Future.

There is A False Cloak to believe that everyone has the Power and Ability to Forgive a Person, this however was Revealed By The Unlimited Mind of The Universe to be just a hope that it is Possible. God Revealed to me that if a person have not found Love or is in Love with a person, then when it is that something went wrong, that brings forth the need for A Spirit of Forgiveness, that person who was Originally not in Love with another person will not be Able to Manifest A Spirit of Forgiveness that sees both parties now letting go of the Past to embrace A Positive Future. Thus it is being Manifested that those who have not Loved, cannot Be in Love, Therefore, they cannot Forgive.

There are Guidelines to be used in the Process of Forgiveness; The Lord Revealed that unless the Necessary steps are taken to actually prevent that which was needed to be Forgiven, to not be able to have a resurrection of that event happening again, then that which was Originally Being Forgiven will actually take place again, and again, and again; because that person who is embracing the thought of Forgiveness have not truly Understood what Love Is.

Love Is not a Red Heart that we see Displaying in Cartoons with A Arrow piercing the center of that Heart; Love is not a Speech by the movement of our lips, neither is Love a thought. But Rather, Love Is Action to Preserve, Love Is Ugly in Its Foundation, to bring forth Complete Beauty and Full Purpose in its Manifestation, without forgetting about The Ugly Foundation; Love Is Rough and causes a lot of Pain, and brings forth a lot of Sacrifices to thus Preserve that which is Loved.

Thus it must be recognized by The Instructions from The Unlimited Mind of The Universe that those who are in The Process of Forgiveness, because of Love, they will establish Walls that prevent the Original Hurt to never take root in their lives Again. This was the case for The Lord, when Adam and Eve Sinned, and Broke God's Commandment. If God Was Never In Love with His Creation to thus Preserve The Future and The Destiny of Mankind, It is a Fact, man would not have only died Spiritually in The Garden, but Man would have also Immediately died Physically in The Garden of Eden, and there would have never been A Salvation Plan for Man if God Was Not In Love with His Creation, to Bring man back to His Glory, that sees God Establishing Forgiveness.

Because of Love, God Set Angels with Flaming Swords to prevent Adam and Eve from entering again into The Garden, to thus prevent them from having access to eat of The Tree of Life, to thus Remain in Sin and to live forever in a Sinful state and a Sinful Body. Therefore, God Placed Spiritual Walls to Ensure that what took place at the beginning of Man's Transgression will never be able to be Repeated; and this was all done in The Spirit of Love to Birth A Fruit Called A Spirit of Forgiveness, which was only Manifested because there was at First The Spirit of Love.

Genesis Chapter 3:22-24.

"And The Lord Said, Behold, the man is become as one of us, to know good and evil: and now, lest he put forth his hand, and take also of The Tree of

Life, and eat, and live forever: Therefore The Lord Sent him forth from The Garden of Eden, to till the ground from whence he was taken. So He Drove out the man; and He Placed at the east of The Garden of Eden Cherubims, and a Flaming Sword which turned every way, to keep the way of The Tree of Life".

Forgiveness is Completely wrapped up In God's Love, and will never be Manifested unless a person Knows about God's Love. Therefore, A person being in a Relationship, if they are not exposed to God's Love, they cannot love their partner, therefore fulfilling this fact, that whenever something takes place that requires the need of Forgiveness, that person will never be able to express Forgiveness because there is no Foundation of Love from God in the life of that person.

Forgiveness paves a pathway for those who are being forgiven to find, and to be placed in their Original Position that they were in. If Forgiveness does not lead back to Purpose Being Fulfilled, then it is not Forgiveness. This was Revealed by The Unlimited Mind of The Universe.

CHAPTER 7

GOD IS TIMELY

Genesis Chapter 18:14.

"Is anything too hard for The Lord? At the TIME Appointed I Will Return unto thee, according to the TIME of life, and Sarah shall have a son".

Galatians Chapter 4:4-5.

"But when the fullness of the TIME was come, God Sent forth His Son, made of a woman, made under the law, to redeem them that were under the Law, that we might receive the adoption of sons".

Ecclesiastes Chapter 3:1-8.

"To everything there is a season, and a Time to every purpose under Heaven: A Time to be born, and a time to die; a Time to plant, and a Time to pluck up that which is planted; A Time to kill, and a Time to heal; a Time to break down, and a Time to build up; A Time to weep, and a Time to laugh; a Time to mourn, and a Time to dance; a Time to cast away stones, and a Time to gather stones together; a Time to embrace, and a Time to refrain from embracing; A Time to get, and a Time to lose; a Time to keep, and a Time to cast away; A Time to rend, and a Time to Sew; a Time to keep silence, and a Time to speak; A Time to love, and a Time to hate; a Time of war, and a Time of peace".

There remains in the Physical part of a man, the Ambitions and Desires of wanting to see fulfilled what God Has Purposed to be Fulfilled within the Lives of People, Nations, and Languages. But this desire still doesn't move The Fixed Destined Purpose of The Set Time that God Must Fulfill what is to be Fulfilled, only in the Time Set for it to be Fulfilled, which is to Manifest God's Glory and Will Being Fulfilled. What this means is that even though it is seen that there will be many that would even seek to help God in fulfilling what is to be Fulfilled, their help will remain at a level, because that which is to be Fulfilled Must Manifest The Glory of The Spiritual God and not the Wisdom of a Physical Man.

Lord, Come Forth Now!
Lord, Do What Is To Be Done In My Life Now!
Lord, Let Your Spirit Move To Manifest What
Is To Be Manifested In My Life Now!
Speak Now Lord, Move And Fulfill Your Promises!

Even with such A Cry from A Child of God, it will be Revealed by The Spirit of God; Comforting Words and Special Touch of Peace to ensure that we are kept on the pathway that leads to that Manifested Time of God's Will Being Done; and if this Cry is made every day, this will still not Fast Track God's Time to be brought forth at an earlier time than that it is schedule to be Established for.

There are many times in our waiting of God's Time, it can be compared to being stifled or suffocated, but there is an Understanding that God Needs to be Born in us, to let us be Knowledgeable that the Level of which we thought we would surely be killed, it remains at a Level that it was only a Shadow of Death that appeared, that desired for us to believe that this is the Environment and the Challenge that is fixed to bring us to our sure end. After we have passed that level that we thought would have killed us; it must be embraced that there are still other levels that The Lord Has Fixed on the pathway of

A Child of God, to thus Manifest that we will Overcome to prepare us for The Atmosphere of God's Timing.

God Is Intentional in everything that God Does, meaning that, no matter how Hot the Fire gets in our preparation of God's Time, the Fire is not set to Kill A Child of God, but rather The Fire is Set to Remodel A Child of God to The Likeness of God's Character; and it must be known that The Fire that Burns to shape our lives Is GOD. The Understanding must be Born in us to become Knowledgeable, that it Is God that Does Everything; the devil has no Power over A Child of God, rather, he is Given The Approval by God to Fulfill Task, but still, it Is God that Grants The Approval for what is happening in the life of A Child of God to Happen. Thus the End Product Will Manifest God's Time for God's Will to Be Done, whether it be Good or Evil.

Job Chapter 1:20-22.

"Then Job arose, and rent his mantle, and shaved his head, and fell down upon the ground, and Worshipped, And said, Naked came I out of my mother's womb, and naked shall I return thither: The Lord Gave, and The Lord Hath Taken away; Blessed be The Name of The Lord. In all this Job sinned not, nor charged God foolishly".

1 Samuel Chapter 3:17-18.

"And he said, What is the thing that The Lord Hath Said unto thee? I Pray thee hide it not from me: God do so to thee, and more also, if thou hide anything from me of all the things that He Said unto thee. And Samuel told him every whit, and hid nothing from him. and he said, it is The Lord: <u>L</u> <u>et</u> <u>Him Do what seemeth Him Good</u>".

CHAPTER 8

GOD IS GOOD

Genesis Chapter 1:31.

"And God Saw everything that He Had Made, and, behold, it was Very Good. And the evening and the morning were the sixth day".

It is Revealed by God to me, that everything that God Has Made to Be Good, it is also Manifested that, that which is Made Good is also Granted The Approval for that which is Made Good to Remain Being Good under that Calling of that which it is made to Fulfilled. This means that Provisions, Influence, Protections, and Inspirations are put in Placed by God to ensure that what is Made for a Specific Purpose, must be fed to maintain that Destined Purpose.

Everything that God Has Made to be Good, if it does not fulfill the Purpose of Remaining to be Good; this will therefore manifest The Divine Purpose of God to Mark that which God Has Made to be Good, then becomes not Good, to be established has an unprofitable Vineyard that was not worthy in the first place to be made for Good to Fulfill God's Purpose. Therefore, All that was Provided for by God to ensure that what He Made Good was Preserved, will be taken away, because the Purpose of Remaining Good by that product is not being Maintained.

Isaiah Chapter 5:1-7.

"Now will I Sing to My Wellbeloved a song of My Beloved touching His Vineyard. My Wellbeloved hath a vineyard in a very fruitful hill: And He Fenced it, and gathered out the stones thereof, and Planted it with the choicest vine, and built a tower in the midst of it, and also made a winepress therein: and He looked that it should bring forth grapes, and it brought forth wild grapes. And now, O Inhabitants of Jerusalem, and men of Judah, Judge, I pray you, Betwixt Me and My Vineyard. What could have been done more to My Vineyard, that I Have Not Done in it? Wherefore, when I Looked that it should bring forth grapes, Brought it forth wild grapes? And now go to; I Will Tell you what I Will Do to

My Vineyard: I Will Take away the Hedge thereof, and it shall be eaten up; and break down the wall thereof, and it shall be trodden down: And I Will lay it waste: it shall not be Pruned, nor Digged; but there shall come up Briers and Thorns: I Will also Command the Clouds that they rain no rain upon it. For the vineyard of The Lord of Host is the house of Israel, and the men of Judah His Pleasant Plant: and He Looked for Judgement, but behold Oppression; for Righteousness, but behold a Cry".

A Good God Only Does Good Things, even though it will seem to those who are not Serving God, that what God Has Done when Destruction comes was not good; but we have got to be Born of the Understanding that God Destroys to Preserve Good. God Makes an example of one Person, People, Nations and Country to Manifest The Fear of God in another Person, People, Nations and Country to thus Maintain The Requirements and Standards of God's Will in that Country.

There are times when we are faced with Sickness and Death, Persecutions and Trials; Forces of Darkness on every side. In all of this, God Is Still Good. We will Observe that whenever we are faced with such Challenges; this type of Oppression springs forth A New Anointing, that causes God's People to Raise The Level of their faith to now be Born in The Belief that Their God Is Good and also Bigger than anything that may ever come their direction. The Secret however is Prayer. The Higher the Oppression, the harder it will Be for A Child of God to Pray. This is the reason why it was Mentioned in The Bible, that when Jesus Christ Prayed, and His Sweat became has Drops of Blood. This was because of the Great Oppression that was before Him; but still He Prayed, Laying down an Example for those of us that are to follow in His Footsteps, to let us know that Prayer Is Essential in A Child of God Victory, no matter what the condition of life Brings, just keep on Praying.

If we can but discover that we are Being Seasoned to Overcome; if we just begin to Acknowledge God in that Atmosphere of our Trials, we will then Discover that we have Climbed into A New Anointing of Grace with The Father Above, that sees us now stepping over all those things which seems to have the power to destroy our Destiny.

**God Is Good, All The Time; And
All The Time, God Is Good.**

CHAPTER 9

GOD IS ALWAYS PRESENT

St Matthew Chapter 28:17-20.

"And when they saw Him, they Worshipped Him: but some doubted. And Jesus came and Spake unto them Saying, All Power is given unto Me in Heaven and in Earth. Go ye therefore, and Teach to all nations, Baptizing them in the Name of The Father, and of The Son, and of The Holy Ghost: Teaching them to observe all things whatsoever I have Commanded you: and, lo, I Am with you always, even unto the end of the world. Amen".

I'm not afraid to discuss The Doctrine of The Church of Jesus Christ Fellowship Savannah Cross Limited. There are many persons that would not even mention this Scripture, because they are not able to explain what is being said. It is Obviously seen that The Lord Said to go and Baptize in The Name of The Father, Son and Holy Ghost; which is in fact The Name of Jesus Christ. But what is amazing to realize is that all the Disciple that went away from that Instruction, all of them upon Receiving The Gift of The Holy Ghost, Knew exactly what is The Name of The Father, they knew what is The Name of The Son, and they Understood what was The Name of The Holy Ghost; and they all Agreed through The Revelation of The Holy Ghost and their journey with The Gospel of God, that The Name Is One, Being The Name of Jesus Christ.

It is evidently recorded in The Bible, that after they Received The Holy Ghost Peter stood up after many confusions of what was taking place by those who were observing The Manifestation of The Glory of God; and He said The Doctrine Is:

"Repent and be Baptized In The Name of Jesus Christ for the Remission of our sins, and ye shall Receive The Gift of The Holy Ghost". Acts Chapter 2:38.

Just have a look, it is there for everyone to read! The Bible Said in Acts Chapter 4:12.

"Neither is there salvation in any other: for there is none other name under Heaven given among men, whereby we must be saved".

GOD IS…

Galatians Chapter 3:27.

"For as many of you as have been Baptized into Christ have put on Christ".

Ephesians Chapter 2:19-22.

"Now therefore ye are no more strangers and foreigners, but fellowcitizens with the saints, and of the household of God. And are Built upon the foundation of the apostles and prophets, Jesus Christ Himself Being The Chief Corner Stone; In whom all the building fitly framed together growth unto an holy temple in The Lord: In whom ye also are builded together for an habitation of God through The Spirit".

1 Timothy Chapter 3:14-16.

"These things write I unto thee, hoping to come unto thee shortly: But if I tarry long, that thou mayest know how thou oughtest to behave thyself in The House of God, the pillar and ground of the truth. And without controversy great is the mystery of godliness: God Was Manifested in the flesh, Justified in The Spirit, seen of Angels, preached unto the gentiles, believed on in the world, received up into Glory".

Come to think about it, was any of the Disciple including Paul, in the Actions of the Apostles, was it seen that any of them did any Baptism beside that being done in The Name of our Lord Jesus Christ?_____
_____.

Paul found certain Disciples in Act Chapter 19. And asked how were they Baptized; after receiving the answer that they were Baptized after John's Baptism of Believing on Jesus Christ, he had to Baptize them all over again, because John's Baptism was only for Belief, not to allow a person to Receive of The Holy Ghost, thus they could not Receive of The Holy Ghost, because The Authority, Covering and Access, which was Only In The Name of Jesus Christ was not there. The Book is there for all to read, let us begin to read, so that we may understand God's Will.

Furthermore, The Bible Said that Jesus Christ Said:

"All Power is given unto Me in Heaven and in Earth".

A Smart person will ask this Question:

If Jesus Christ wasn't God, then how could He Have Declared that He Has All Power in Heaven and in Earth; because we know Who it is that Has All Power, and that Person Is God.

Note: The Lord throughout all ages has Demonstrated that He Is One God, and also that He Is A

Jealous God; God Have Demonstrated that there are No gods beside Him, He Knows not any; no one Dictates to Him, No one Instructs Him. Then how is it, that Jesus Christ Being His Son, now Acknowledge that He Is In The Position of God, if He was not that Eternal God, that Manifest Himself to a Lower Level, and Call that Anointing His Son, which came for the only Purpose to Die for the Sins of Mankind.

Furthermore, whenever it is explained by any religion expressing who they have revealed God to Be, if you would listen very carefully, there is not an explanation that can be given by any Religion that can separate God from Jesus Christ and Jesus Christ from God; because that explanation does not exist. Jesus Christ Said:

"I and My Father are ONE".
St John Chapter 10:30.

My focus wasn't really The Baptism, but seeing that this Scripture mentioned Baptism, I was compelled to assure My Readers that I'm also prepared to discuss Baptism with the facts, and not a theory.

The Lord Said: "And, lo, I am with you always,
even unto the end of the world. Amen".

There are many Conditions and Situations in life that make us wonder at times if God Is Still Present in what we have found ourselves to be experiencing. And this part of The Message is a reminder that God Promises Never Fails; His Presence Never Fails to Exists.

I'm a living Testimony, and am sure that there are many before me, that can make the same proclamation that God Never Fails; and even when it seems like He is not with us, He's just Standing there, to Watch Us Overcome that which we think we can't Overcome. It is also observed that God Is Not Going to Move when we desire for Him to Move; but Understanding must be born in us to know that God Moves to Fulfill His Glory, therefore, Patient we must Become.

CHAPTER 10

GOD IS JUSTIFIED

What does it really mean for God to Be Justified?
_____.

According to The Oxford English Dictionary, the word Justified derives from the word Just, which means to be right and fair; deserved; we all get our just deserts. The Nelson Illustrated Dictionary of The Bible has the words Justice of God, which States:

"God's Fair and impartial Treatment of all people. As A God of justice, He Is Interested in fairness as well as in what makes for right relationships. His Actions and Decisions Are True and Right. His Demands on Individuals and Nations to look after victims of oppression are Just Demands. As Lord and Judge, God Brings Justice to Nations and sets things right in behalf of the poor, the oppressed, and the

victims of injustice. For the wicked, the unjust, and the oppressor, God as Supreme Judge of the Earth Is A Dreaded Force. But for all who are unjustly treated, God's Just Action is reason for Hope".

There are many Stories in The Bible that Reflects God as A God of Justice; one such Story can be found in The Book Judges Chapter 19–Chapter 21. In summary The Tribe of Benjamin did an Immoral Act which was observed by all the other Tribes of Israel has a Sin that needed Immediate judgement; therefore, They called for those who were responsible for the despicable Act; this was rejected by the Tribe of Benjamins, this caused all the other Tribe of Israel to gather themselves and to take the decision to war against the Tribe of Benjamin, of which they also consulted God, and The Lord Told them to Go Forth because they will be Victorious.

The Lord Also Told them to let The Tribe of Judah to go up first. They Obeyed The Voice of God to Let Judah go up first, and they were destroyed on two occasions. It was later observed by The Children of Israel that God Is A Just God; meaning, if God is Asked to Judge, is God Going to be Partial in His Judgement, or is God Going to Judge Israel as a whole? Because in God's Eye, Israel Is One, just as how He Is One, Therefore, If Judgement was to be Administered for The Tribe of Benjamin, all Israel would have to be Placed on God's Measuring Scale.

The Tribe of Judah which was considered to be God's Law Giver had to be Judged First, because they were the People that Knew God's Councils and Laws to Perfection, therefore, The Lord Asked them to go up First, so that He Can Judge Them First. And if Judgement comes in the form that your own people would Kill you, then all in all. That's God's Judgement Being Established upon that Individual's Life.

When The Tribe of Judah Recognized that it was within The Laws of God for their Tribe to Bring God's People to a State of Cleansing and Submission before God that their Sins Will Be Forgiven By God, it was not until then, they discovered that The God of Israel is in no way partial towards Judgement and Justice. After they came before God and was Cleansed, they were now Able to Receive of God's Spiritual Approval for Justice to be brought on The Tribe of Benjamin for that Disgraceful Sin that The Benjamites did.

This Example in The Bible Should Bare witness for all who would require for God to Judge, or to Bring forth Justice upon the Land or in the lives of People, Nations, Languages and Dominions; if God Is Going to Judge, which means to Bring forth Justice, then The Church Must Brace themselves for the Impact of God's Judgement to be Done to them first, because Judgement Must Begin with those who are Knowledgeable about what God Words Ask us to Fulfill. After The Church Is Judged and Now Made Clean, and is again A Holy

Example for all to Follow, then God Will Then Move unto the Physical establishment that is in charge to keep the Laws of the land in place that Justice will be done for all People, Nations and Languages. In a nutshell, Spiritual Establishment Must Be Judged before Physical Establishment Are Judged. That Is God Being Justified, agree or don't agree, that's The Facts.

Another Example of God Being Justified In The Bible is The Story of Jonah with The people of Nineveh. According to The Spiritual Laws of God, The City of Nineveh Must Be Destroyed to Bring Forth God's Justice based on the fact that Nineveh Committed Great Sins and continued to do those Sins. But the moment The City of Nineveh Changed from that which they were doing to Anger God's Action to Bring Forth Justice; that Change in The Direction of The People brought forth A Unique Mercy in The Order of God's Justice, to Prove that Once Repentance Has been Acquired, God Is Still Justified In not Fulfilling that which was Deserving to take place within the lives of People, Nations, Languages and Dominions.

CHAPTER 11

GOD IS MERCIFUL

Psalms 18:24-27.

"Therefore hath The Lord Recompensed me according to my righteousness, according to the cleanness of my hands in His Eyesight. With the merciful thou wilt shew thyself merciful; with an upright man thou wilt shew thyself upright; With the pure thou wilt shew thyself pure; and with the froward Thou wilt shew thyself froward. For Thou wilt Save the afflicted people; but wilt bring down high looks".

St Matthew Chapter 5:7.

"Blessed are the Merciful: for they shall obtain Mercy".

St Luke Chapter 22:39-43.

"And one of the malefactors which were hanged railed on Him, Saying, if Thou Be Christ, save thyself and us. But the other answering rebuked him, saying, Dost not thou fear God, seeing thou art in the same condemnation? And we indeed justly; for we receive the due reward of our deeds: but this man hath done nothing amiss. And he said unto Jesus, Lord, remember me when Thou Comest into Thy Kingdom. And Jesus Said unto him, Verily I Say unto thee, Today shalt thou be with me in paradise".

For many of us, Mercy is a word that at times cannot be Understood or Explained, as it at times seeks to contradict the very existence of what the word Justice stands for. How can a person explain when a man Have committed a Sin, and it is well known the type of Sin that this man has committed, that he by his own actions is worthy of the full Measure of The law to be executed upon his own life; then suddenly The Lord Steps In and Said for this man's life I Grant Mercy; all that he has done is now washed away, because I Give Myself in his stead.

Adam's Fallen Race was already deemed worthy of Death, we deserved it, but God Stepped In because of Love for His Creation, to Know what is our full Potential without Sin in His Presence, and God Said: I Will Die so that man may Live, Mercy. We don't deserve it, but

GOD IS...

Mercy. We don't Understand it, But Mercy; We do not know what we will be doing for The Kingdom of God, but God Knows, and He Declare and Decree A Word Called Mercy.

The Balance of life, both in The Spiritual and Physical Dictates that sin have been committed by Man, thus death is the Punishment; but God Paid the price that no one else could pay, and Declared Mercy, because He Foresees that Man Will Return to his Rightful place of being UPRIGHT to stand before The Eternal Spirit of God.

Mercy Is Already Granted for all Mankind by The Fulfillment of The Death of Jesus Christ, The Manifestation of God in the Flesh; then what is the difference between the man on the cross accompanying Jesus Christ to His Death, and one of Jesus Christ own Disciple Named Judas?

The Difference was that the man on the cross recognized that he was wrong and was worthy of the Punishment of Death, he asked for Reconciliation, Received it through Mercy; while on the other hand, Judas Recognize that he was wrong just by speech, he never sought Forgiveness, but went away, committed suicide, relinquishing himself from the pardon of Mercy; because it is a Fact, if he did not Kill himself, then Mercy would have also been his Reward if he had truly Repented of his sin. But everything is already fixed, as it was already prophesied that such would be the destiny of the person that betrayed The Lord.

St John Chapter 8:1-11.
"Jesus went unto the mount of Olives. And early in the morning He Came again into the temple, and He Sat down, and Taught them. And the Scribes and the Pharisees brought unto Him a woman taken in Adultery; and when they had set her in the midst, They say unto Him, Master, this woman was taken in Adultery, in the very act. Now Moses in the law commanded us, that such should be stoned: but what sayest Thou? This they said, tempting Him, that they might have to accuse Him. But Jesus Stooped down, and with His Finger Wrote on the ground, as though he heard them not. So when they continued asking Him, He Lifted Up Himself, and Said unto them, He that is without sin among you, let him first cast a stone at her. And again He Stooped down, and Wrote on the ground. And they which heard it, being convicted by their own conscience, went out one by one, beginning at the eldest, even unto the last: and Jesus was left alone, and the woman standing in the midst. When Jesus Had Lifted up Himself, and saw none but the woman, He Said unto her, Woman, where are those thine accusers? Hath no man condemned thee?

She said, No man, Lord. And Jesus Said unto her, Neither Do I condemn thee: Go, and sin no more".

I hope that we've discovered that one of the Main Medium through which a person is deemed worthy of Mercy's Escape from their conditions that leads to their deaths, is to first identify within ourselves that, that which we were accustomed to perform, that caused us to be in a State of Continual sin before God's Eye, is the same Condition of sin that we must now be prepared to Kill, in order to receive of Mercy's Favor. If Sins Door is not Closed, then Mercy's Door will never be Opened to Accommodate those who are attempting to Close The Doors of Sin Forever. Both cannot Exist, it's either we continue to Sin and be shut out from Mercy Forever, or we've decided to Kill Sin, which causes The Door of Sin to be Closed, then to Receive of The Access of Mercy's Door, A Favor Released from The Father Above.

CHAPTER 12

GOD IS WORTHY

Growing up with My Grandfather and Spiritual Father, The Late Bishop Austin Whitfield, His life as A Testimony made me realize the Great Value of how Great God Is, and also to know that God Is Indeed Worthy to Be Served. I got a firsthand View of the life of Bishop Austin Whitfield, His Dedication to The Work of God, His No Nonsense Behavior towards Church and also and most Important, His Personal Relationship He Had Developed with His Savior. For Example, I remember coming from school on a certain day, and it was customary that I knew that once the Bishop had his door Closed, it simply means that he was either Reading His Bible or He was in Prayer with God. I took it upon myself one day to open the door of Bishop Whitfield in one of those moments, and I was met with an Immediate Rebuke. Bishop Said and I Quote:

"Out of order and Disrespectful: Don't you see that I'm Talking with My Lord!"

It was later explained to me again by Bishop and Lady Whitfield, to understand that whenever I see the door Shut, I must understand that Bishop is having Relationship with God, therefore, I Must never disturb him while he is having his communication with God.

I learned a lot from Bishop Whitfield's life with God, some of which I never understood why he was so Humble to Fulfill all that God Would have for him to Fulfill. Meaning, there are times Bishop went to Church and did not receive any offerings, but that did not stop him from coming the next day or the next day. Some days he only received that which could only buy a quarter of Bread, and still he was persistent to make certain that he was in another Prayer Meeting Service. This confused me, because I was attending School, and was very Good at Mathematics, therefore, When I calculated what Bishop was doing to his body and for The Service of God, it didn't add up, it makes no sense! This caused me to take a closer look to discover what was the real reason for this man doing all these Sacrifices, and still there are no Physical Rewards. I Discovered that when there was a Service where someone Received The Gift of The

Holy Ghost, Bishop was now overflowing with Joy, not a joy because offering was collected, but rather, because someone was Born into The Kingdom of God. He would often Say:

"Do you Know what this means for me? One more Star within My Crown In Heaven".

Bishop Austin Whitfield Walked to Church, and the journey was not short. At a point in His life that he was no longer able to Serve, upon pronouncing God's Blessing of Favor on The Ministry that I must now Bare, He had this Advice to give to me:

"Minister Dinnall, Just Give God A Clean Work, and You Will Be Ok, No One Can Touch You, Once You Give God A Clean Work. God Bless You My Son".

Bishop Austin Whitfield made me Understand that nothing in this Whole World must prevent A Child of God Service for God's Glory, because God Is Worthy to Be Served. No Money, No Man, No Woman, No Opportunities, No Heights, No Depths, No Principalities, No Powers, No spiritual wickedness in high places, Not even the devil himself, let nothing stop your Purpose because God Is Worthy.

Revelation Chapter 4:6-11.

"And before The Throne there was a sea of Glass like unto Crystal: and in the Midst of The Throne, and round about The Throne, were four Beasts full of eyes before and behind. And the first beast was like a Lion, and the second Beast like a Calf, and the third Beast had a face as a man, and the fourth Beast was like a flying Eagle. And the four Beast had each of them six wings about him; and they were full of eyes within: and they rest not day and night, saying, Holy, Holy, Holy, Lord God Almighty, Which Was, and Is, and Is to Come. And when those Beast give Glory and Honor and Thanks to Him that Sat on The Throne, Who Liveth Forever and Ever, The Four and Twenty Elders fall down before Him that Sat on The Throne, and Worship Him that Liveth Forever and Ever, and cast their Crowns before The Throne, Saying, Thou Art Worthy, O Lord, To Receive Glory and Honour and Power: for Thou Hast Created All Things, and for Thy Pleasure they are and were Created".

CHAPTER 13

GOD IS THE BEST CHESS PLAYER

It is certain, according to Bible Studies, and by the Mouth of the wise king Solomon, that there is absolutely no searching that can be done that would effectively find out the Nature and the Order in which The God of The Universe thus Move to Fulfill that which is His Intention to be Fulfilled within His Own Councils. As The Bible Says, No One Counsels God or tells Him what to Do or when to Do to Manifest What He Intends to Do to Fulfill Mysterious / Unsearchable Purpose.

It is found that many have Identified that God Had Accomplished a Miracle for His People in a particular Fashion, but that demonstration still does not determine that God Will Again Move in that same Direct Order to Fulfill a similar Miracle in another Child of God life, because the situation of the Problem is the same. God

GOD IS...

Has to Prove and Manifest Himself to Be The Only Unstoppable Force In The Entire Universe, thus God Is Always Creating New Ways to Fulfill Miracles and Breakthrough For His People. One of the Main reasons for this is because of the plans of the enemy. The enemy will always seek to Study the lives and the pattern in which God Has Delivered for His People, to thus prevent a Similar Deliverance for God's People at another time.

There is found in The Bible that God Commands His People at Time to Fight, and then at another time God Commands His People that they will have no Need to fight in the Battle because the Battle is not theirs, but it is The Lord's Battle. There are times The Lord Command for His People to fight in the Plain that confuses the enemy to think that God's Strength is only in the Valley, thus when the order of the Battle is set upon the Mountains, God Proved Himself Strong Upon the Mountains to Demonstrate to all People, Nations and Language that there is Absolutely No god That can be Compared to The God of All Seasons, Locations and Conditions.

It is found that many will plan to Kill, Destroy and put in Bondage the lives of God's People; but when they are planning to do all these things, The God of The Universe Steps In, and Reveals Secrets that were spoken in the bed Chamber of His People's Enemies, to let His People Know Exactly where to Go and where not to Go, thus preserving the lives of those who Trust in Him.

King David never moved to fight in a Battle unless he had The Permission of The God of All Strategies to Direct his way Forward. And even when the signs of Movement were so strange to Observe, he Waited, and was Obedient towards The Voice and Instructions of The God that Sees Everything.

CHAPTER 14

GOD IS NO RESPECTER OF PERSONS

One main Example of this fact is the story of Adam and Eve. While there are many Stories that can be given as reference within The Bible, all these other Stories were a Diluting of the Character and The Glory that Adam and Eve had before God. Adam was made after The Likeness of God, meaning that he was made to stand Upright Before God and not be found Unworthy to Stand before The Full Manifested Presence of God. Therefore, When it was Observed that Adam Sinned; God Did Not Hesitate to Fulfill that which He Said He Would Do. This should let us understand that if God Had No Respect to those in The Spiritual, then those who are of the full manifestation of Flesh must observe Sleep and Mark Death. If We Do Not Do God's Will, It's A Certain, there will be no Pardon for us.

This was also Observed in Heaven, when Lucifer conceived in his Mind that he was going to build his kingdom above The Most High God. Being then a Spiritual symbol for The Manifestation of God to Bring forth Glory to God, not even this brought forth a state of Respect Within The Mind of God. The Lord Sent His Word and Rebuked Lucifer, Erasing his place forever before His Eyes.

Let us not Find out if God Will Respect Us to Pardon us when we do something wrong. Let us not plan to sin, but rather when we sin, let it be a Mistake, that we will repent of and learn from the Mistakes, that we will not make the same mistakes again. Because God Is No Respecter of Persons.

CHAPTER 15

GOD IS JEALOUS

To explain this Topic is to Understand that God Is Demanding of everything and every Purpose that He Has Made His Servants to Fulfill, which means that if God Created A Child of God to Fulfill The Purpose of Becoming A Pastor; there is absolutely nothing that such an Individual can do beside that of Pastoring, to Fulfill God's Just Desire for God's Purpose to be Done in The Lives of those who are Called and Chosen to Manifest that Purpose.

The only person that could become an Abraham was only Abraham, because of the Calling and The Purpose that was to be Fulfilled over His life, which God Demands to Be Fulfilled over His life. Abraham was already Formed and Designed with all the Ingredients to Fulfill God's Purpose. Saints should never worry, because God Being Jealous is a Good Thing, because this

Jealousy Drives Divine Purpose to Be Fulfilled from His Servants, which sees God Milking such an Individual for the exact type of Service that is Required By His Will to Be Fulfilled. And nothing and No One can over Power God's Jealousy, because it is directly tied into God's Will Being Done. David Had to Be king of Israel, it was being set in Motion long before David was even Born, that Purpose was structured in the life of Ruth to marry to Boaz, which were David's great grandparents.

Jonah Found out that God's Purpose and Jealousy was so Great that it overcame every personal Decisions that a person may ever have to Fulfill for their personal desires. When A Child of God Life Demands Service for God, that Child of God has to be very careful of what they even eat, what they speak, where they go, who they have company with, because anything that seeks to destroy Purpose for God, Will and Must Bring forth God's Jealousy. And be Warned, No Servant of God would desire for God to Activate The Movement of Jealousy over their lives; do what God Requires for you to Do and Be for His Glory and Will Being Done. Therefore, Be Warned!

CHAPTER 16

GOD IS PATIENT

It was Revealed to me by God to demonstrate this part of the Topic in this way. Imagine being in sin far away from God, but yet still even though it has become our practice to remain in sin, because God is understanding of what our future will hold, He Remains Patient, though at times we deserve death from the actions we commit. God Is Found Always Considering what we can become and that which we will become despite the sinful body of that which we were. There are many times we become frustrated because we just have not seen what God is Doing in The Spiritual to fulfill that which should take place in our lives Physically.

There is another way to consider this Topic: Being God's Children it must be born in our understanding to know that God is Destined to take care of all the needs of His Children, thus God Does in fact has a set Time Table which schedules His Timing has to when He Will Move to Speak to Create that which is Divinely Fixed for each of His Children. There are many times we would desire for God to speed up that which is destined for us, but we need to also understand that our schedule time for our Blessings from God is also tied into someone else having received their Blessings that will automatically pave the way for us to be Blessed.

One of the foundational ingredients is to understand that God in His Ultimate Form Is Spiritual, therefore when it is that God Requires for Blessing to be manifested within the Physical, the Chosen Vessels Are Used to Fulfill God's Desired Purpose in the Physical. The Word of God Would Allow for us to Understand that those without us could not be made perfect, this was said to make us understand that we could never make it by ourselves, it needed the foundation of those before us and contribution from those that will come after us to enable us to reach the prize of the Higher Calling in God; hence we are subjected to always Pray, Fast and Grant full support for our Brothers and Sisters that is Serving God just the way we are Serving God, to see them through, that they will experience the Breaking of the day of God's Divine Favors. Likewise, they themselves have to be Born in the Attitude that they also have the Relationship with God that Manifests over their lives that they see themselves also Praying, Fasting and Supporting other Sons of God to receive their Deliverance from The Hands of God.

I'm often explaining to The Church that when God is in the process of Blessing a person within The Church, that all the other members of The Church must be in a Mind frame that they themselves are also Blessing that person, because any other thoughts from that of blessing for your fellow Brothers and Sisters will result in the sin that is called INIQUITY. And because the sin of Iniquity has been committed by many of God's People, this causes God's People to be destroyed because of our Ignorance towards our own spiritually infected sins of which God Will Never Answer our Prayers if we have not Repented of that Sin which we have committed within the Spiritual.

My advice to the Readers is to Trust In God, then being Patient on God's Timing will be Easy.

Numbers Chapter 23:19.

"God is not a man, that he should lie, neither the son of man, that He should repent: Hath He Said, and shall He Not Do it? or hath He Spoken, and shall He Not Make It Good?"

What do you think; Is God Going to Fulfill What He Has Promised You? _____
_____.

I often repeat these words to The Saints of God to allow our Minds to be at ease when it concerns God's Promises; This is what I always repeat:

"If God Has Spoken Words of promise to His People, we need not to worry, because the moment He Spoke those Words, it was Already Fulfilled in His Time. If He Knew that He Wasn't Going to Fulfill What He Said, then He Would not have Spoken that which He Said".

Isaiah Chapter 55:8-11.

"For My Thoughts are not your thoughts, neither are your ways my ways, Saith The Lord. For as the Heavens are higher than the Earth, so are My Ways Higher than your ways, and My Thoughts than your thoughts. For as the rain cometh down, and the snow from Heaven, and returneth not thither, but watereth the Earth, and maketh it bring forth and bud, that it may give seed to the sower, and bread to the eater: So shall My Word be that Goeth forth out of My Mouth: it shall not return unto Me void, but shall Accomplish that which I Please, and it shall Prosper in the thing where to I Sent it".

CHAPTER 17

GOD IS IN ALL NATIONS, CULTURES AND TONGUES

One of the biggest mistakes that Mankind has made and continues to practice the manifestation of their mistake is to think that The God of The Universe is subjected to only one set of people. This was Revealed to me by The Unlimited Mind of The Universe to be an error, has it is for those who have received my Message called The Nature of God, in this Message it Reveals that God Gave me A Vision that Establish the clear Fact that He Is In All Nations, Cultures, Languages and Dominions.

It is important for us to understand this reality, because as it stands many are actually breaking God's Spiritual Laws because they have been born in the Belief that God Is Separated from some People and Nations, and His Will is with only a select set of people. There are many things that man have position himself to manifest what must be selected or engrafted by God Himself, and because we've stand in The Position against God's Will so many times, it brings forth a great misunderstanding of what is God's Will Being Done, because it has now become man's rules and desires being fulfilled.

The Lord Reveals to me that for all Nations, Cultures and Languages, there is a Fixed Ten Percentage of the people that Belongs to Him, that must be engrafted in The True Will of God that His Kingdom will be Established, and in His Kingdom there must be Representative from all Cultures, Nations and Tongues to Manifest and Acknowledge that Jesus Christ is The True and Living God, The Lamb that was slain from The Foundation of the World.

Malachi Chapter 1:11.

"For from the rising of the sun even unto the going down of the same My Name Shall Be Great among the Gentiles; and in every place incense shall be Offered unto My Name, and A Pure Offering: for My Name Shall Be Great among the Heathen, Saith The Lord of Hosts".

It must be understood that the Gentiles were considered to be the Heathens of God's Covenant of Peace that God Had with The Children of Israel, which means that they never knew how to Please The Living God. But in this Scripture God Has Identified that it shall be, even if it was not taking place in the current atmosphere of The Gentiles giving Honor and Glorifying God; The Lord Prophesied by the mouth of Malachi to make known that it shall happen and must happen, that even those countries that knows nothing about The True and Living God, even a remnant of that Country that Represent The Tithes of the land unto God, they must know and be Born in The Understanding to become Knowledgeable of what kind of life is Acceptable unto The King of kings and The Lord of all lords.

Galatians Chapter 3:8.

"And the scripture, forseeing that God would justify the Heathen through Faith, preached before the Gospel unto Abraham, Saying, In thee shall all Nations be Blessed. So then they which be of Faith are blessed with Faithful Abraham".

The Qualified State that Abraham Had Acquired to attract The Manifestation of The Living God upon his life and the lives of his generation, this type of Covenant Blessing was not limited to only the direct seed of Abraham, but it is a Fact, that this Covenant Promise was an example established for all Nations, Cultures and Tongues to Understand that there Is A God that Requires Special Attention from our lives unto Him to thus Manifest within our lives and the lives of our generation the same undiluted Covenant of Peace which was Established upon the life of father Abraham and his descendants has long as they and also for us to remained in The Will of Almighty God.

Psalms 148.

"Praise ye The Lord, Praise ye The Lord from The Heavens: Praise Him in the heights. Praise ye Him, all His Hosts. Praise ye Him, Sun and Moon: Praise Him, all ye stars of light. Praise Him, ye Heavens of Heavens, and ye waters that be above the Heavens. Let them Praise The Name of The Lord: For He Commanded, and they were Created. He Hath also stablished them forever and ever: He Hath Made A Decree which shall not pass. Praise The Lord from the Earth, ye Dragons, and all deeps: Fire, and hail; snow, and vapour; stormy wind fulfilling His Word: Mountains, and all hills; fruitful trees, and all cedars: Beasts, and all cattle; creeping things, and flying fowl: Kings of the Earth, and all people; princes, and all judges of the Earth: Both young men, and maidens; old men, and children: Let them Praise The Name of The Lord: for His Name Alone Is Excellent; His Glory is above the Earth and Heaven. He Also Exalted the horn of His People,

the Praise of all His Saints; even of the children of Israel, a people near unto Him. Praise ye The Lord".

Please take notice of this Psalms: Was it not written by Inspired men of God and sent to all People, Nations, Cultures and Tongues?_____.

Thus this Psalms Establish the Fact that God Is Mindful of All People, Nations, Cultures and Tongues. And it is evident that The Manifestation of The Almighty will be Established from the lives of all People, Nations, Cultures and Tongues because we all make up The Full Body of Christ by Obedience through His Will Being Done in our lives.

Let us stop from judging other Countries because within the secret of their Relationship with The Father will be Revealed for another country how to overcome a manifestation of the spirits of devils that keeps a whole lot of other people bound under the influence of the power of the Atmosphere that seeks to bar us from The Mercies of our Heavenly Father. Help one country to get closer to God and that other Country will Reveal Secrets to another Country of how to get closer to God, because God Can Be Found In All People, Nations, Cultures and Tongues.

CHAPTER 18

GOD IS THE UNKNOWN

There are many times even Christians are confused and fearful of that which is uncertain and appears to be The Unknown, but a True Child of God will discover through Relationship with their Savior that once we have been born in the Attitude and Spirit of Trust for God, this Relationship will become our Active Passport to Walk, Run, Praise and Worship our way in every environment which presents itself to be Fearful, Uncertain and Unknown, because our Father Is The Foundation of Everything that is Unknown. Before there was The Heavens and The Earth, there was God, and He was Unknown to everything that He Created until He Decided that He Was Going to Create these things. Everything that was Created that came from God was Unknown, and everything will return back to God's Will Being Done in The Unknown. Therefore, we begin with

GOD IS...

The Unknown, then Creation, Time Manifested, and Time Fulfilled, leads to God's Destined Kingdom in a Dispensation without ending of God's Unknown.

Noah was told to build an Ark to prepare for The Unknown Storm, although being Mocked, Jeered and Talked about in disbelief, he believed in The Unknown of God's Word. Abraham was told to separate Himself to seek for The Unknown, he believed in God and moved directly into a Famine that could have shaken the Foundation of his belief in The Unknown, but he stayed focused because The Unknown Brought Forth Relationship that could not be denied. Moses was called to lead God's People in The Unknown, at times he himself needed the assurance of The unknown to continue on the journey that The Unknown Asked them to walk in. Ruth was determined to follow her mother in law to The Unknown, her Stubborn Character to follow after the evidence of The Unknown God enabled her to become The Fixed Destined Great Grandmother of the man David who was found to be a man after God's Own Heart. Esther being fueled with faith that she was going to present herself to the king to save her people, she was well aware that if the king did not call for her to be in his presence she could have been put to death. But Relationship with God Overpowered every unknown threat of a physical man, thus she stepped with boldness not considering her own life, but knew that The Unknown God Was Always With His People.

I will encourage God's People to be Born in The Understanding that without Faith it is Impossible to Please God, for he that cometh to God Must, Must, Must believe that God Is A Rewarder of All People who Diligently Seek for His Face in The Unknown Manifestation of this Physical life.

CHAPTER 19

GOD IS IN IT

There are many things that have happen to us, that we would love to know the explanation of why such a thing did happen; but even with the most Brilliant Minds, we are left in a state of confusion, because we just cannot Understand how to connect the dots with the physical training we've come to now depend on to be our guide of explaining why things happen when they do happen. It is in this state of Mind that many will come to the clear Fact, that there is A Bigger Intelligence at work than all the Intelligence there can be found upon the Earth Combined. And it is with this consideration that those who are Wise, will now be Born in A Attitude of Humility, to Co-operate their whole life to The Leading and Guidance of The Unlimited Mind of The Universe.

Have you ever been in an experience that what is currently taking place in your life, is completely out of control for you to manage, but in the same breath, because of Obedience towards The Direction of The Spirit of God, that which is seen has out of control to your limitations, is Now in Complete Control of The God that Steers your Journey. And this experience is what God Needs for us to be comfortable in, to know with Full Assurance that God Is In It.

Here is an Example to show how Great God Is. This is not My Testimony, but I play a Major role in this Testimony.

My Mother always gave her Testimony in Church, to show how Great God Is. She explained that she grew up in Church, seeing that her mother and father were both Christians, but somewhere along the road of her Christianity in her early twenties, she declared that the devil tricked her to believe that there was better in the world for opportunity, than that was in The Church. She got pregnant and lost her way from God, and was now in a state that she believed that there was no way back to God, because of how deep in sin she had become. Tears came to my Mother's eye whenever she testified to say: But God had A Way to Use the child that she was pregnant with, to be a Teacher and a Preacher, to thus encourage her path back to God. God Created A Way out of no way, that no one could imagine that God Was and Still Is The Plan for every Believer.

This may not be your Testimony, but still it serves a purpose to let us know that God Is In Control of every path that A Child of God should ever take. God Has A Way to Administer The Test, just to let each Believer Be Born with A Testimony, thus making us know that there is no better life than the life that God Has Given for us to Walk In.

The Lord Reveals that His Plans and His Will for those who are already Fixed to Inherit Heaven is so Strong that not even the actions of sins can prevent that person from entering The Gates of The City; because He Has Already Paid the Price of all Sins, therefore, He Already Has The Power to Redeem those who are Trapped in sin, that seems to have no way to find themselves out of Sin.

The Lord Reveals that those who have Fallen to the Traps and Snares of Sin that are Fixed for Heaven, are those who He Will Restore, to thus Train and Teach those to come after us of their Experience and their Testimony of what they had encountered, so that those who are to continue after us will have a living prove as Testimony, to show what they are not to be a part of, to therefore prevent the same mistakes from taking shape in the lives of those who art to move towards Perfection. Therefore, It is already in God's Will for many that walks this Christian's Pathway, for us to actually get Burned, become Broken, Battered, Abused and Mistreated; for A Testimony, to declare to others of how Good The Mercies of God Truly Is.

The Lord Reveals that if we are Truthful to Him in everything that we could ever encounter, then in the same breath, God Will Be Truthful to us, in every Direction that our lives carry us to Fulfill our journey to Enter Heaven. It is in the meaning of the words, Relationship with God.

Galatians Chapter 5:7.

"Ye did run well; who did hinder you that ye should not obey the truth?"

Exodus Chapter 14:19-25.

"And The Angel of God, which went before the camp of Israel, removed and went behind them; and the pillar of the cloud went from before their face, and stood behind them: and it came between the camp of the Egyptians and the camp of Israel; and it was a cloud and darkness to them, but it gave light by night to these: so that the one came not near the other all the night. And Moses stretched out his hand over the sea; and The Lord Caused the sea to go back by a strong east wind all that night, and made the sea dry land, and the waters were divided. And the children of Israel went into the midst of the sea upon the dry ground: and the waters were a wall unto them on their right hand, and on their left. And the Egyptians pursued, and went in after them to the midst of the sea, even all Pharaoh's

horses, his chariots, and his horsemen. And it came to pass, that in the morning watch The Lord Looked unto the host of the Egyptians through the pillar of fire and of the cloud, and troubled the host of the Egyptians, And Took off their chariot wheels, that they drave them heavily: so that the Egyptians said, Let us flee from the face of Israel; for The Lord Fighteth for them against the Egyptians".

CHAPTER 20

GOD IS NOT IN IT

1. Iniquity
2. spirit of Envy
3. Covenant Breakers
4. Malice Keepers
5. spirit of Wrath
6. Disobedience
7. Deceivers
8. Distractions
9. spirit of Covetousness
10. Confusions
11. Contradictions
12. Complainers / Murmurers
13. Boosters
14. Doubters
15. Liars
16. Thieves

17. Perverse persons
18. Pretenders / Hypocrites
19. Prideful Minds and Hearts
20. Divinations
21. Enchanters
22. spirit that soweth Discord among Brethren
23. Haters of Good Things
24. spirit of Mischief
25. Peace breakers
26. Those that destroy the family circle
27. Oppression

And these are only a few of the Things that God Will Not Associate Himself with.

CHAPTER 21

GOD IS BALANCE

There will never be one set of power and force to be activated within this world that the end product will not realize that God is Going to Step In to Allow for The Rightful Order of that which is to happen in life to now be fulfilled. From the beginning of time to the very ending of time, Balance will always be established and maintained because our God Reflects that which is Balance. Righteousness will always stand FIRM and Unrighteousness will always Exist for this present life, and whenever time it is that unrighteousness has received it's full share of dominance because of The Punishment that God Has Granted Access for what to take place in the lives of People, Nations, and Cultures, whenever time expiration date has arrived for punishment to stop, then the season of Righteousness, Turning back to The Will of God will again be Activated and Born in The Generation of those who have Positioned themselves for a NOW walk of Righteousness in God's Rule.

There are truly many more things that God IS, these are just a few that come to mind, that The Lord Allowed for me to write about, to Encourage His People to keep on holding on to their Faith in God.

Remember that God Can Never Forget about His Children because we are indeed A Reflection of His Word and His Will Being Done, therefore allow this Manuscript to be a constant Reminder to our Souls of what is The Foundation of Who Our GOD IS.

Let Us End With Prayer...

"Lord Jesus Christ, I Thank You, that I was found Worthy to be Used by Your Spirit, to Inspire Your People on This Christian's Pathway. I Pray that this Message Will Remain to be A Pillar of Strength for all those who will read, that they will become stronger in the Faith, to always Believe that You Are In Everything that is Impossible, that Moves to Your Will Being Fulfilled in the Lives of Your People. Accept All Praise for This Message, because this is Your Mind, I'm only Your Tool. In The Name of Jesus Christ, To God Be All The Glory, Great Things He Has Done".

To The God that IS and IS and IS; Jesus Christ The Lamb of God, All Glory, Honor and Praise be unto His Name Forever to Eternity, Amen.

From The Ministry of The Church of Jesus Christ Fellowship Savannah Cross, Jamaica, West Indies. God Bless. Pastor Lerone Dinnall.

GOD IS ALL That You Need Him To Be On This Christian's Journey. Just Believe!

God's Spiritual Laws...

Message # 98	Date Started June 25, 2018
	Date Finalized June 27, 2018.

To The King of kings and The Lord of lords, The Only Unlimited Mind of The Universe, Jesus Christ The Lamb of God. I Greet all God's Wonderful People in none other Name but The Name of Jesus Christ; Privileged it is for me to again find myself in this Position to write Inspiring Messages for God's Children.

    I Believe that each Message is geared towards Releasing An Anointing for the Season that A Child of God must find themselves to endure, in order to Overcome that which the Season brings forth. Let this Inspiration be in the Minds of God's People, that there is always a Level of Anointing that is waiting to be Released for God's People to be victorious over everything that the enemy decides to afflict The People of God with, that being the Burdens that we face.

    It is well documented in The Bible The Laws of God to man that mankind and his generation will forever be in good standing with The God of The Universe; that which I'm speaking of is none other than The Ten Commandment that was Given to Moses and The Children of Israel. They are as follows: Exodus Chapter 20.

1. **Thou shalt have no other gods before Me.**
2. **Thou shalt not make unto thee any graven image.**
3. **Thou shalt not take The Name of The Lord your God in vain.**
4. **Remember the Sabbath day, to keep it Holy.**
5. **Honour thy father and thy mother.**
6. **Thou shalt not kill.**
7. **Thou shalt not commit Adultery.**
8. **Thou shalt not steal.**
9. **Thou shalt not bear false witness against thy neighbor.**
10. **Thou shalt not covet.**

These Ten Commandments is The Foundation of Spiritual Laws, The Binding Contract between God and Mankind, that will ensure that God Will Grant Favors and Release Blessings on those who Follows and Teach their children to Follow the same guidelines of that which The Lord Has Commanded for Mankind to **KEEP**.

It is recognized in the Laws of the land that many Countries will now seek to Institute Laws for their people that will no doubt reflect that which The Laws of God Have Demonstrated; by doing this, it will be considered to be very wise for the Countries, Nations and Languages that have taken The Councils of The Most High God to Be A Tradition.

It is needless to identify that the Countries, Nations and Languages that do not reflect The Characteristics of The Laws of God, those Countries, Nations and Languages will no doubt find themselves to be building on Sinking Sand; which means that whenever it is the time for the Storms of life to pass, these Countries, Nations and Languages will not be able to stand the passing Storm which is **A MUST**.

It is currently being experienced in the lives of those who are Serving God a Great Decease of Fear that is being implemented by those who have no Idea of Who God Is to His People and most important What God Will Do to Bring Vengeance upon those who have unnecessarily brought Bondage and Afflictions upon the lives of God's People. It is Reported in The Bible Which Says:

**"If The Foundations be removed,
What shall The Righteous do"?**

It is also Said in The Bible that Heaven and Earth shall pass away but My Words Shall Not Pass Away. The Word of God Is The Foundation of Life; and those who have The Word of God Living in them is no doubt The

Living Manifestation of God Himself In them. Therefore, whenever it is challenged or put to the Test for God's People to be Destroyed; this Test will Manifest The Great Deliverance of The Supreme Ruler of The Universe to now Step In, Show Up, Show Off, Dictate what will now be the Future of those who have their Foundation to be The Likeness of Spiritual Laws.

I have experienced for myself great Burdens and Afflictions that seem to have no end. A constant reminder at all times of what this World and the Laws of this World Decides to Dictate upon those who are Serving The Living God, and that's to implement the belief system in those who are living now and for those who are to continue in our stead, that being our Generation to follow. And this is the Fear and the Law that the Nations, Countries and Languages seeks to Imprint in the Minds of those who are living now; to let us believe with all our Heart, Soul and Mind to be born in the belief that whatever we have Received from God Has A Blessing is not ours to retain, meaning that this World will now seek to Manipulate The Minds of God's People to believe that their Laws and their Customs which is in complete contradiction to what The Laws of God Have Demonstrated is of more importance than that which God Has Laid Down as Spiritual Laws.

There are many times even Christians Look to the Hills from whence cometh their Help, to Ask God if He Does Not See what the enemy is doing to put in Bondage those who Trust and Obey that which God Asked us to Continue in. And this is where we need not for the spirit of frustration to take effect in our lives, because if we truly knew The Words of God, we would have Identified that all Iniquity that People, Countries, Nations and Languages, that which they would have piled upon their own heads would first have to be full in the Vessel that God Has Designed to be full.

Now when the Vessel of Iniquity is now Full for those who seeks to put in Bondage and Slavery those who Serve God, No amount of Money; No Power that is Instituted by the Laws of man; No Fame; No Protection; No, No, No, there is No Escape for those who have put in Bondage those who are Serving The Living God. And that's The Bible Speaking.

God Will Not Manifest Judgment on those who Oppress His People until The Cup of Iniquity has been full and now running over. Therefore, For those of us who Understands The Words of The Lord and Understands Spiritual Laws; the name of the game is Patience; just wait a little while longer, endure the Threats and Abuse. And if we have truly been born in The Understanding to know Spiritual Laws, we will no doubt Understand that whatever the enemy seeks to do to us, there is always A Barrier of Protection, that what they can mostly do is only to speak words of Threats of that which they intend to do, but it's a fact, they really cannot fulfill that which they have spoken to fulfill.

Genesis Chapter 15:12-16. This passage of scripture makes mention of God Speaking to Abraham letting him know that his generation shall be in bondage for many years, but in the fourth generation God Shall Bring them forth from slavery. But have a look at the ending of verse 16, when The Lord Was Making Abraham know that this action for his generation to come out of bondage and possess that which is Promised by God will only take place at a particular time when the Iniquity of the Amorites is now full. At this time God Will Release Judgment upon the people of the land and the Instrument that God Will Use to Judge those who are filled with Iniquity is those who are Walking in The Righteousness of Spiritual Laws.

Exodus Chapter 3:19-22.

"And I Am Sure that the king of Egypt will not let you go, no, not by a mighty hand. And I Will Stretch out My Hand, And Smite Egypt with All My Wonders which I Will Do in the midst thereof: and after that he will let you go. And I Will Give this people favour in the sight of the Egyptians: and it shall come to pass, that, when ye go, ye shall not go empty: But every woman shall borrow of her neighbor, and of her that sojourneth in her house, jewels of silver, and jewels of gold, and raiment: and ye shall put them upon your sons, and upon your daughters; and ye shall spoil the Egyptians".

It is important for God's People to be Born in The Understanding to Know that we as a People can never come out of Bondage unless we have now decided that we are fully going to follow The Requirements of God's Spiritual Laws. Therefore, The length of time that we take to move forward from Bondage to Spiritual Freedom truly depends on our decisions to Change direction from a walk of darkness to a walk of God's Likeness. Here is a Fact that many will not want to hear:

"Many of God's People are currently in Bondage because of the Sin we continue to perform".

The Truth Hurts but it is necessary!

Spiritual Laws in comparison to that of Man's Law; The Bible Truly Identifies that if the Laws of the Land are in agreement with the Laws of God, then all people must now align themselves to make sure that we are Obedient to that which the Laws of the land asks us to fulfill. But what if the Laws of the land are in Complete Contradiction to that which The Laws of God Demonstrate? Should we still be Obedient to that type of Law, seeing that those Laws will now shape our Destiny, and The Destiny of our Generations?

_____.

And this is where The Children of The Living God needs to Identify the misdirection of man and his Laws, that will no doubt spring forth The Divine Protection of God's Spiritual Laws upon those who Trust in God. In Man's Law whoever they decide that should lose at what time they have fixed for that person to lose, must be fulfilled because they have made it a law which means that it carries weight and can be brought to full manifestation or so they think. It is like their playing a game of Chess; they've become the Judge, the Jury and the Executioner; because they have moved their desires and Intention to take over and destroy that which The Righteous have; they really believe that it will be made possible, just like Haman that build the Gallows for Mordecai and The Children of Israel to be destroyed in one day.

The laws of man have Doctrinated their beliefs to think that they can have their own ways and rules over God's Inheritance. Let me use this Message to Sound the Alarm for all those who actually think that God Is Going to Leave The Righteous in the hands of the Egyptians; because of a Truth, the Laws that are currently being practiced are that which the Egyptians exercised. **Wake Up!** These Actions and These Laws never worked in the Past for God's People, why do you believe that it will work in the Present or in the Future, **Wake Up!**

Spiritual Laws Dictates that if One Righteous person must LOSE; then all Unrighteous people would have already LOST. Spiritual Laws Dictates that if A Righteous person must be Judged then all Unrighteous People, Countries, Nations and Languages would have already been Judged. Spiritual Laws dictate that if A Righteous man must Die by the councils and laws of man which is outside of The Directions of The Will of God for that person to die, then it would mean that all men who are Unrighteous along with their generations would have already been put to Death. That is Spiritual Laws.

"Please take into consideration that this is speaking of A Righteous Person in God's Eye".

Therefore, We will identify that at many times when we are put under Oppression by those who seek to oppress us; it is not that they actually have The Power to Oppress God's People; but rather because God's People are just not knowledgeable of what God's Word Ask of us to Know, therefore, We find that we by ourselves have Chained our Feet to that which Man's Law have dictated that we should now become.

"My People Are Destroyed because of a lack of Knowledge". Hosea Chapter 4:6.

It is found at present that there are many Assigned Demons that are Fixed to Plague the lives of God Chosen People; the people which are not yet Knowledgeable of the Fact that if we are **AWARE** of what Spiritual Laws Dictates, these Demons that have filled the Vessels of people who we even know, whatever Message they have brought to further Inflict additional Oppression on

God's People, these Messages or Seeds will have no effect on a person that is Knowledgeable of what God's Word Dictates, which Reveals The True Power of Spiritual Laws.

Demons do understand True Authority, and Demons knows The Voice of God that comes forth out of A Child that is living for God. And when it is that these Demons have sent forth their servants with duties that must be fulfilled; whenever the Message comes back to that Demon from the servants that they have sent forth, to let them know that the person that they are assigned to put under Oppression, have Manifested A Voice that is Unique above all voices, and the resemblance of that Voice sounds like the same Voice that Spoke in the beginning of time, that Said:

"LET THERE BE LIGHT"!

Because the Demons are knowledgeable about Spiritual Laws, these demons will now back off from what they were doing to a person that has now Manifested, that they are A Son of God, that is no doubt, under The Protection of The Most High God. And this Protection is always:

"Touch not The Lord's Anointing nor do His Prophets any Harm".

It is also mentioned in The Bible, God's Divine Protection on those who believe in The Living God.

St Matthew Chapter 18:6.

"But whoso shall offend one of these little ones which believe in Me, it were better for him that a millstone were hanged about his neck, and that he were drowned in the depth of the sea".

Demons will do everything in their power to remain in the vessels in which they possess because demons are spirits, which means more than one spirit, and these spirits cannot manifest unless it has a body for those spirits to Manifest in; therefore, When it is found that a Demon is now threatened by The Living Authority and Voice of God, this demon or demons would now consider very carefully on how they now deal with A Child that is Living for God. Because if it is Attempted that these Demons try to put in effect that A Child of God should suffer or be place in Bondage; then that which will now be Released is The Constitution of Spiritual Laws, which will now require for the very person in which the Demon has Possess to become the first person in line to lose all that they have, and also that Demon which possess that body will be seeking for a new vessel, because in Spiritual Laws, you just cannot **TOUCH** that which belongs to The Almighty God.

There is truly Level to know about God and His Spiritual Laws; if it has not been Revealed to you by God, then the Fact is, that you cannot walk in The Anointing of what God Is Releasing each day for those who are walking in God's Will.

Starting this Journey to Build an Altar for The Name of The Lord Jesus Christ, there are certain Spiritual Laws that The Lord Would Allow for me to Understand so that on this Journey I will always be Protected by His Anointing. And many may wonder why I'm able to write many things of Mysteries that speaks to a lot of forces that are indeed affecting God's People, and yet still these forces have not the power to hurt me or to stop that which God Has Asked of me to write on paper for His People to know; this is all because of God's Divine Protection upon my life.

One of The Spiritual Laws that God Reveals is to make me know that I must always be Respectful especially to those who bares The Office of The Lord, whether it is in my opinion or not, if they are living a life for God; The Command Was Given that I Must Respect The Office of The Lord.

There will always be those who believe that they can say and do anything to a person that is walking in The Anointing of an Office that God Has Given; this however carries great consequences for those who are purposed of not being Knowledgeable of The Protection that surrounds a person that Wears The Title and Walk in The Office of The Lord.

The Office of The Lord Carries The Authority of The Lord; therefore, It would be advised for those who are being Instructed by A Pastor, A Bishop, A Priest, A Minister, or A Missionary, to make certain that all that is asked for that person **to fulfill within Spiritual Laws,** to make certain that, that which is Commanded, is carefully carried out. Because the fact is, if we Disobey God's Office, it means that we are Disobeying God's Councils; of which, when we are in Disobedience to God's Spiritual Laws there is nothing that can protect us anymore, because The Spiritual Brings forth the sure Manifestation of that which should take place in our lives Physically.

A Servant of God Needs only to make certain that they Warn, Preach and Teach; Prophesy to those who God Asked them to be of service to, whether that person decides to receive the

Message or not, The Officer of The Lord has freed Himself from the burden of that which should befall those who have not taken heed to The Message that was Delivered.

There can be no Deliverance for those who have willfully determined themselves to make certain that they break God's Spiritual Laws; the Breaking of Spiritual Laws carries consequences that must be fulfilled in the lives of those who have broken A Spiritual Law. And many times there is found that a person have broken A Spiritual Law in one Area of their lives, and it is that same person that will seek The Blessing from God from another Priest in another location, to counteract the effects of that Curse; to think and believe that God is separated from The Spiritual Laws that He Has Instructed. And it will be observed that no matter how hard that other Priest, Pastor or Bishop Prays for a person that has broken Spiritual Laws, that person would have to bear the punishment for the Law that was broken before there can be any further Deliverance. Now I know that there will be many persons that will not believe what is being Revealed, but The GodHead Has Revealed, and I Move and Write according to what God Has Revealed.

Another important Spiritual Law is that Tithes and Offerings, of which those who have not Separated themselves unto Holiness will never be able to Experience The True Divine Blessing that will be Released from The True God of The Universe. What this means is that it's not everyone's Tithes and Offerings is Accepted by God, but rather The Tithes and The Offerings that will be Accepted is that which has the Ingredients of Separation which leads to Holiness; and Freewill, which means that you weren't forced to give, but rather because of the gratitude of the heart towards God and His Work, this person has made The Choice to Release to God's Work Freely.

Iniquity is another Spiritual Law that Cripples Especially God's Children, because many will believe that the goal of Christianity is just to present themselves outwardly to be A Christian, of which this is completely False. But Rather to be A Christian starts from the Inside and then it has its Reflection on the Outside.

Iniquity speaks of spiritual unclean thoughts that a person conceives to entertain within their mind, of which they think that because it remains in the spiritual, there will be no effect of those thoughts in the Physical.

Once the Mind is entertaining Iniquity, then the Heart of a man **Must Fulfill** that which the Mind is feeding the Body with; because it is The Spiritual that moves The Physical. The first place that judgment begins to take effect is in The Spiritual Were God Dwells, and when it is that God Now Moves His Spirit to Erect Judgment, the spiritual part of a man is what God Looks on First.

Therefore, Many Pretenders of Christianity are actually Sieved Out of God's Divine Deliverance and Blessing, because there is found in them The Constitutional Error of Spiritual Laws being broken. Christians that are filled with Iniquity will become like The Children of Israel in Isaiah Chapter 58, who really thought within themselves that outward manifestation will reflect Spiritual Manifestation; of which, if we are not Directed by God, this will lead to us serving God for many years, and still will never be able to experience The Divine Deliverance of The Almighty God.

Another Spiritual Law is that of Gain; there is Righteous Gain and there is Unrighteous Gain, of which The Righteous Gain will lead to life filled with The Blessings of God Almighty, the unrighteous gain will lead to a life of sinful imprisonment.

There is found in the World at present that there are a lot of Institutions Namely: Government Laws; Banks; Credit Unions; National Housing Developments; Private Entities etc. And their requirement for gain to allow the Country and Businesses to actually exist, is to Burden their people and clients with demands that are in complete contradiction to that of Spiritual Laws.

Note: The only Requirement by Spiritual Laws for Gains that God Always Require from the hands of His People is only and has always been **10%**, and this is the Requirement from The Unlimited Mind of The Universe, which Established the Foundation of the Past; Knows the Present and Fulfills the Destiny of the Future. And God Requires **10%.**

Note: There is no Mind that is Bigger or that can Outshine The Mind of God. Now have a look very carefully on that which is going to be Revealed Next. The Bible Declares and it is also found in the beginning of this Message The Foundation of Spiritual Laws which begins with The Ten Commandments that was given to

Moses and The Children of Israel. Now within the first two Commandments God Said:

1. **Thou shalt have no other gods before Me.**
2. **Thou shalt not make unto thee any graven image.**

Now the point I'm trying to make is this: If The God of The Universe Requires only **10%** of everything that we Are, that we Earn, and that which we can Give as Talent and Worship to Him, then, do we not understand that every and any other Force and Institution that requires more than that which God Has Required is indeed the same voice, thought and spirit of **ENVY** that was found in Eternity, that wanted and desired to build his kingdom above The Most High God. Do you not see for yourself that the Councils and the Governance of these Institutions are in fact being Led by the prince of this World that being the Devil himself! These Institutions have caused many of God's People to actually Break Spiritual Laws; because Spiritual Laws Says:

**"Thou Shalt Have No other gods before Me".
And "Thou Shalt Not Make Unto
Thee Any Graven Image".**

We have not only made these gods to prosper for years, but we've also been feeding and sustaining these spirits that has their leader to be the prince of this World, who is in Fact Lucifer, the Devil himself. The evidence is clear that all can see, these Institutions are asking for Gains of that which outshines that which God Has Required, thus Manifesting the spirit of Envy which says:

"I Will Build My Kingdom Above The Most High God".

When we go to these Government Offices, the Banks and Credit Unions or any other Financial Entity, are their Requirements for receiving a loan within the area of 10%, No, No, No! They are rather asking for a Gain above 10%. Some of them are asking for 15% for an Individual to receive their money to do business to be able to live on God's Land; some Institution is asking for 18.5%, some is asking for 25%, some 30% and upwards. And if we are not careful, the time will come that these Businesses and Government will ask that we sign our Souls over to their will, for them to release benefits for our lives.

And the real Sin that these Institutions have bound upon us is that they require these Percentage of Gains every Month. If you have a bad season the requirement is fixed; if you're sick and in the Hospital for months and cannot pay your bills, this is still a requirement for that bill to be paid.

And here comes the Greater Sin, don't forget about the Interest-rate for the loan that you have Borrowed, and if you cannot pay at the time Required, these Rates Are Compounded each day to further bury a person that Has Broken Spiritual Laws.

God's Requirement for Tithes and Offerings is not to put Bounds and Chains for those who should Give, but rather God Has Generated The Requirements of Freewill for all those who will give back to God at an Accepted time for that person to now Freely Give.

Another Spiritual Law is that of Separation, whenever A Child of God Has Truly Separated themselves and have now Tasted of what it now Truly means to Be Holy, then that Child of God Has to Become Discipline so that they can in fact Maintain a life that Represent The Holy Characteristics of God, because if this is not Maintained, then Spiritual Laws would have then been broken, which will result in The Protection of God upon that Child of God's life to be Removed, thus we are exposed to any and every danger that should come our way.

Another Spiritual Law is that of Invitation, which means that those who are Invited within your surroundings are indeed those who have been given the permission by you the person that has Invited them to spread that which is of their own Characteristics and spirits. Therefore, Be very careful of this Spiritual Law, because if it is found that A Child of God Is Separated for Righteousness, and that Child of God Invites someone within their surrounding of which that persons Manifestation is not of God, then that person who have done the Invitation will receive Punishment whether they are knowledgeable of this action or not; it doesn't take away from the fact that A Spiritual Law was Broken.

There is one other Important Spiritual Law that needs to be brought to light for God's Children to know, which is The Authority of God upon the lives of those who are living for God. Spiritual Laws Dictates that if a person truly Seeks The Face of The Living God, then that Journey will Reveal and must Manifest The Anointing of God Almighty upon the lives of those who Trust in God. Therefore, It is of great necessity that each Child of God Seeks The Face of God for themselves, to know God not only by someone's Testimony or through songs, but to know God **PERSONALLY**. Let knowing about God be your song and your Testimony, let it be your very life that you live.

These are but just a few of The Spiritual Laws, these are Permitted by God to be Revealed to Empower His People to further Search The Scriptures to Unlock The Hidden Mysteries, which will allow Demons and the Devil himself to back off from the lives of those who are calling upon The Name of Their God. And in case you do not know the Name of Your God, His Saving Name Is **JESUS CHRIST**.

May The God of Heaven and Earth Continue to Bless and Prosper the lives of those who have read this

Message, and I Pray that God Will Reveal to you more of His Spiritual Laws so that each Child of God Will Be Equipped with The Armor of God to Stand up against Principalities, Powers, Works of Darkness, and especially the Fear that the Enemy will seek to Inject within the Lives of God's Inheritance; this I Declare and Decree In The Mighty Name of Jesus Christ.

From The Ministry of The Church of Jesus Christ Fellowship Savannah Cross, Jamaica, West Indies. God Bless you from Pastor Lerone Dinnall.

Abide Within The Walls Of God's Spiritual Laws.

Missing Spiritual Steps!

Message # 133   **Date Started May 16, 2020**
                        Date Finalized May 16, 2020.

Proverbs Chapter 3:5-10.

"Trust in The Lord with all thine heart; and lean not unto thine own understanding. In all thy ways acknowledge Him, and He Shall Direct thy paths. Be not wise in thine own eyes: fear The Lord, and depart from evil. It shall be health to thy navel, and marrow to thy bones. Honour The Lord with thy substance, and with the firstfruits of all thine increase: So shall thy barns be filled with plenty, and thy presses shall burst out with new wine".

Greetings family of God in The Name of Jesus Christ our Soon Coming King. It feels good and blessed to be in this position another time to bring forth Glory, Honor and Praise to The Father of The Universe. I'm thanking God daily for this privilege of still being connected to

GOD IS...

The Source of all Strength, the Whisper of A Voice, The Movement of The Spirit of God, The Burning of The Holy Ghost, The Approval to write and not to look back and wonder if that which I've written is in accordance of God's Will Being Done, because The Spirit of God Bears Witness at all times for that which The Lord Approves for me to write. Therefore, there is no spirit of anxiety or fear within my vessel to cause me to wonder if this is God's Will Being Done.

    I met with someone yesterday, this person I've always seen when I enter a particular business place but have never spoken to this person before. I got A Vision from God with different business, meaning the Vision was not one but the Vision speak to a lot of things and touched on a lot of topics, while going through the Vision I saw a picture of this person and The Lord Said:

"Speak to her and tell her that I have Need for her service in My Kingdom".

    When I approached the person and told her what The Lord Told me, she was in denial of what I saw in the Vision. I then expressed to this person that this wasn't a request from me as a Pastor nor do I seek for her to be a part of my Assembly, but this request is coming from The Only Authority that Exists and it wasn't a Request from God but rather it was a Command. The person said to me that if I get the Vision again I should let her know. I told her that The God that I serve don't need to send me to her again because the Message was already delivered, I Told her that God is not short of Vessels to use, if there is someone's attention that God need to have, then that person is going to know that God Needs their Service. I told her to pray about it and see what unfolds in the life of her family towards this Vision from God.

Missing Spiritual Steps, there is a Level within The Spiritual that only God Alone can Approve to bring A Child of God above the powers and the authorities that exist upon Earth, to Allow that Child of God to See and Discern the full table of life to know the moves of each player before that player even knows the move that they will make in this life. And that Level of Anointing or Authority is called The Spiritual Eyes to Discern the Beyond or Spiritual.

God Teaches A Child of God about The Soul of a man and also Teaches that Child of God about spirits and the effects of spirits when it is invited within the temple of any person. Therefore being Trained by The Ruler of all spirits, A Child of God will become 100% effective in knowing how to identify the movement of spirits and also the direction of spirits.

It is seen that within the training process that whatever A Child of God have missed out on of not being aware of certain movements of spirits, that God The Trainer will summarize that particular day to that Child of God to Identify to that Child of God of what could have been done differently to advance A Child of God's Movement within The Spiritual for what is to be fully achieved from The Spiritual for that particular day.

What The Lord is Identifying in this Message is the fact that each day that is presented to A Child of God is Already Released with The Approval from God with The Movement and Speed in which God has Released that Approval to be received by A Child of God, but the fact still remains that A Child of God that is not yet Trained by God will always lose Spiritual Steps of that which is already Approved by God.

We are often caught in the web to believe that we by ourselves can fulfill the mission of walking through a day to receive that which is Released for us from God within a day to have. This mindset is at fault with every other spirits that has entertained such a thought within our vessel. We are rather always Granted The Approval by God to even sleep and then to arise from sleep, and if we have found ourselves to Master Spiritual Steps, then it will be identified within that vessel that this is a person that can achieve all that God Has Released for that Child of God to have within that day based on the speed of that Child of God to Move. Movements is the first Manifestation of The Spirit of God, without movement every other Characteristic of The Spirit of God is dead within that vessel.

I find myself in God's Training of Movement whispering a little prayer that goes like this:

"Lord, Let Thy Will Be Done".

The reason for this is because within Movement of The Spirit of God there are certain territories and guarded environments that The Spirit's Character of Movement will Pull, Push, Burn to go, of which that new environment is one that you wonder to yourself if you have Full Access from God to enter that circle, because every circle or environment carries the governor of that circle and environment of which if The Authority that is within A Child of God is not strong to overcome the governance of that environment that means that A Child of God will now become a Slave to their new master which governs that environment. And being A Child of God it is very Clear from God Who it is that must remain Sovereign.

It is important to point out in this Message that Movement by A Child of God must be carefully weighed first before advancing to full speed of that which A Child of God seeks to move in, Spiritually first then manifest into physical, because at all times A Child of God has to be aware of that which is called Spiritual Transfer. Therefore it is seen that Acknowledgement to God and Approval from God must become a practice that is done at the beginning and ending of every Step of Spiritual Movement. We cannot have both paths of Spirit's Direction. If we've missed The First Step, then every other step within that day is already crippled.

WARNING!

Different people are always a major factor in Missing Spiritual Steps, because with different people comes the manifestation of difference in people, which speaks of difference in spirits, which means different altars, which means different beliefs of the Operation of God or gods, which equal difference in the Movement of Spiritual Steps. You will see for yourself that many people that are associated with a specific group or circle, their Spiritual Steps are always hampered based on the spirit that has the governance of their circle.

People are not harmful, it's rather the spirit that governs them is, which always leads to the adoption of the rule of that spirit. When seeking to become Perfect in Spiritual Steps, be careful of people with different altars, they are even more dangerous than those people that have not come to the knowledge of knowing an altar.

Let Us Pray...

"Father of Heaven and Earth we come before Your Present in The Name of Jesus Christ, we Give You All Glory, Honor and Praise. Father, we seek always Your Spiritual Guidance that will enable us always to walk in Your Spiritual Steps. God, we acknowledge before Your Presence that there is none like Thee, and we look to You always with expectation in our eyes

for Your Divine Guidance which will spring forth Your Accepted Glory for our lives. Father, we are completely Dependent on Your Spirit to Move before we for ourselves even desire to move, because we are knowledgeable that if Your Spirit Does not Move, then we should not move because there is no Leading of The Spirit of God for us to Move. Father, we Desire everything that is within Your Supermarket for us to have in a day, and everything that we should not have within a day, Father, we ask that You will keep it Far away from us. Father, Protect us from the altars of spirits that will only confuse and stop us from gaining mileage in Spiritual Steps. Father, we give You the permission to continue to Train us in The Spirit that we will never Miss a Step for Your Will Being Done in our lives. Father, we pray that You Will Continue to Remove the limitations from our minds that we will continue to be Focused on Your Approvals. Father again we offer All Praise, Honor and Glory to Your Name Jesus Christ. Amen".

From The Ministry of The Church of Jesus Christ Fellowship Savannah Cross, Jamaica, West Indies. From Pastor Lerone Dinnall, God Bless.

Missing Spiritual Steps!

Tomorrow…

Message # 156 **Date Started September 14, 2020**
  Date Finalized September 14, 2020.

Greetings again to God's Wonderful People, I'm gracious to find myself in this position to fulfill Eternal Purposes for God's Kingdom. To The Almighty God Be All Glory, Honor and Praise through The Exalted Name of Jesus Christ, Amen.

Tomorrow, what do we truly know about tomorrow? _____.

We know through experience that it exists whether or not we have found ourselves to be in preparation for that destined future, the facts remain that it is there. Man's reality and peace is that of controlling what they would require to establish, not only for the present but for the future of tomorrow. Tomorrow speaks of a wide base of which it's manifestation is always uncertain of what will happen next in the mystery of The Invisible Surity of The Spiritual Tomorrow.

Tomorrow, what does it mean?_____
_____.

While tomorrow will bring forth the comfort of what is happening today may end, it still filters and links the sure remnant of what took place in the past, the present, to cement A Tomorrow. Tomorrow is not just for the immediate day but for the continuation of such days with the ingredients of what those days were filled with being the manifestation of who we truly are in the current day activities. Therefore, tomorrow will always present a type of hope for the individual that is Spiritually concerned about what seed is being sowed in their today's life. And that's the true hope of an uncertain Tomorrow, it is flexible according to The Spirit's Direction of that person's acceptance.

Choice, a description known to the world to a person making a decision that leads to a direction, this is known by The Church as Free Will, God's Loanership to mankind of choosing their own path without the direct intervention of His Destined Approval. This is done through The Divine Wisdom of The Father to Establish His Final Kingdom; a man must choose for himself his own destination.

While it is that what is currently taking place in the world would seek to destroy the views of a person's tomorrow, it must be understood Spiritually that the world of today will always be threatened by tomorrow's future. A Child of God should never be 100% focused on that which is being manifested in the world's today but rather become Spiritually Focused on what is taking place in The Heavens for tomorrow, because it's not what man really concludes of what will be a person's tomorrow but it's rather the final decision of The Eternal Father to Eternalize His Divine Plans for a manipulated world design.

I've learnt something about securing the uncertainty of tomorrow that The Lord Revealed to me, this is it:

"Within everyday that is faced by A Child of God this Child of God must seek to sow A Good Seed to at least one person that they have come in contact with for that one day, even if it is found that you don't know this person, that person may be your Angel for that day to secure and release something for your benefit for a future that no one really sees and knows what exactly is going to take place".

It's rather a gift that God Has Allowed to be born within the life of A Child of God, if it's not happening on the inside then the reality is that it can never be established on the outside. Many times we miss the true value of sowing a seed and continuing to sow good seeds to wherever we go and to whomever we meet, the seed will not grow for the initial tomorrow but the seed will certainly grow for tomorrow. Another thing that The Lord Revealed within my Spirit is this:

> "Wherever A Child of God goes to earn money within a Parish or a Location, that same Child of God must also bless that Parish or Location with the same percentage of that money of which they have earned".

I asked The Lord why, and this is what The Lord Says:

> "Every Location in which A Son of God Travels, that Location is Governed by My Spirit or Angel that guards that environment, if A Son of God goes to different Locations or Parishes to conduct business to earn from that business, then A Son of God MUST understand that My Spirit or Angel of that Environment Grants them Access to Earn from that environment, therefore A Son of God being Trained in The Precepts of God MUST understand that once Divine Approval is Granted, then Divine Approval MUST be Appreciated for the continued Access to Earn from that same Location or Parish.

Yes, I know it is going to be said that God's Spirit or an Angel cannot use money, that's a statement for people who are just mean and remain in want's approval for this life. The Bible demonstrates to us in The Book of St Matthew Chapter 10:11-13.

> **"And into whatsoever city or town ye shall enter, inquire who in it is worthy, and there abide till ye go thence. And when ye come into an house, salute it. And if the house be worthy, let your peace come upon it: but if it be not worthy, let your peace return to you".**

The Lord Revealed to me that I **MUST** always seek to bless a business or a person that is within that Location or Parish that I have traveled to for the purpose of earning to thus maintain A Spiritual Balance of Tomorrow's Continual Earnings……. This is the secret that only God Can Approve for His Children to know what it takes to sow Spiritual Seeds into an Invisible Future.

Let's explain how powerful today's seed is for tomorrow's future. When I was working at Stewart's Auto Sales about sixteen years ago, I was a Master Technician then that was given the responsibilities of an apprentice and sometimes two for the main purpose of training these apprentices to become future master technicians. I went to The Kingston Wharf to assist someone to clear some barrels in the year 2018, upon assisting this person through the process I heard someone from a distance shouting: Master Technician! Master Technician! Master Technician! I never responded to the call because that company also employs Technicians for their business, therefore I never thought the call was mine to answer. The person caught up to me and said: Master Technician, and greeted me, and reminded me of his time with me at Stewart's and also thanked me for writing a good report for him to be able to secure a good job at that location, this person also told me that everywhere he went he always mentioned how good I was to him and how I taught him all that he asked to learn and never withheld any information from his knowledge so that he can now be in a good job. I Looked on him and acknowledged that I indeed remember our time at Stewart's Auto, and I'm Happy for how he came out, I said to him:

"Just Continue To Give God The Glory Because It Was God That Allowed You To Be In My Life For That Time, So, Give God The Glory"!

Tomorrow, a person will never really know what will be the effects of Tomorrow without accepting the opportunity of today to continue to sow good seeds. Another thing to understand about tomorrow is that tomorrow continues to grow beyond the current expectations of today. Therefore A Wise Son will look to see Spiritual that his current existence will never and can never remain the same because tomorrow is always speaking of a higher level that always outshines the current today. A wise Investor we must now become because tomorrow is coming even if we're not ready for it.

Tomorrow also speaks to us as Christians of a sure and final comfort from our Father Above, an hope that No One, No People, No Nation, No Country, Systems, Rules, Governance and Powers is able to change, and even if these authorities are combined throughout all dispensations and times, they will still not be able to conquer the sure and final future of a tomorrow in God's Beautiful Kingdom because our God Is **ALMIGHTY**.

St John Chapter 14:1-3.

"Let not your hearts be troubled: ye believe in God, believe also in Me. In My Father's House are many Mansions: If it were not so, I would have told you. I Go to Prepare a place for you. And if I go and prepare a place for you, I Will Come again, and Receive you unto Myself; that where I Am, there ye may be also".

Allow these Eternal Words to grow in our very existence and it will not matter to us what this world is manifesting for it's tomorrow because the world's tomorrow can never be A Son of God's Tomorrow because they both flows in opposite direction, the world's direction and future is always going down to hell; The Sons of God Direction and Future is always Growing Up towards

Heaven's Kingdom of Eternal Life with our Father Above. Remember that!

Let Us Pray…

"Father of Heaven and Earth, In The Name of Jesus Christ Receive All Glory, Honor and Praise from Eternity to Eternity. Father, Your Words Declare that man ought always to pray and not to faint. Father, I Thank You for this Divine Access to Pray, I Thank You for Teaching Your People Spiritual Things that we will be able to master the uncertain future of the world's training. Father, I Pray that You Will Continue to Grant The Access for our minds to be strong in You that we will forever find ourselves hoping in You to maintain for our future that our Faith in You will never die. Father, Keep Your Children Strong in You because the world teaches daily that there is no God, but we Your Sons know for certainty that there is A God because You Live in us and Lives in our children and for their children in this unpredictable world. Father, I Pray that this Prayer will enter into Your Ears for acceptance, this I Pray In The Name of Jesus Christ, Amen".

To The God of The Past, Present and Future Be All Glory, Honor and Praise in The Name of Jesus Christ, Amen. From Pastor Lerone Dinnall and The Ministry of

The Church of Jesus Christ Fellowship Savannah Cross, May Pen, Clarendon, Jamaica, West Indies. Blessing Continually.

Remember, It's Always Tomorrow's Divine Victory For Today's Good Seed...

Write your Personal Revelation from God, add your Special Touch to your Book from this Ministry.

1. _____
2. _____
3. _____
4. _____
5. _____
6. _____
7. _____
8. _____
9. _____
10. _____
11. _____
12. _____
13. _____

GOD IS...

14. _____

15. _____

16. _____

17. _____

18. _____

19. _____

20. _____

21. _____

22. _____

23. _____

24. _____

25. _____

Closing Scripture

Exodus Chapter 15:1-21.

"Then sang Moses and the children of Israel this song unto The Lord, and spake, saying, I will sing unto The Lord, for He Hath Triumphed Gloriously: the horse and his rider hath He Thrown into the sea. The Lord is my Strength and Song, and He is Become my Salvation: He is my God, and I will prepare Him an Habitation; my father's God, and I will exalt Him. The Lord is A Man of War: The Lord is His Name. Pharaoh's chariots and his host hath He Cast into the sea: his chosen captains also are drowned in the Red sea. The depths have covered them: they sank into the bottom as a stone.

Thy Right Hand, O Lord, is Become Glorious in Power: Thy Right Hand, O Lord, hath Dashed in pieces the enemy. And in The Greatness of Thine Excellency thou hast overthrown them that rose up against Thee: Thou Sentest forth Thy Wrath, which consumed them as stubble. And with the Blast of Thy Nostrils the waters were gathered together, the floods stood upright as an heap, and the depths were congealed in the heart of the sea. The enemy said, I will pursue, I will overtake, I will divide the spoil; my lust shall be satisfied upon them; I will draw my sword, my hand shall destroy them. Thou Didst Blow with Thy Wind, the sea covered them: they sank as lead in the mighty waters.

Who is like unto Thee, O Lord, among the gods? Who is like Thee, Glorious in Holiness, Fearful in Praises, Doing Wonders? Thou Stretchedst out Thy Hand, the Earth swallowed them. Thou in Thy Mercy Hast Led forth the people which Thou Hast Redeemed: Thou Hast Guided them in Thy Strength unto Thy Holy Habitation. The people shall hear, and be afraid: sorrow shall take hold on the inhabitants of Palestina. Then the dukes of Edom shall be amazed; the mighty men of Moab, trembling shall take hold upon them; all the inhabitants of Canaan shall melt away.

Fear and dread shall fall upon them; by The Greatness of Thine Arm they shall be as still as a stone; till Thy People pass over, O Lord, till the people pass over, which Thou Hast Purchased. Thou Shalt bring them in, and plant them in the mountain of Thine Inheritance, in the place, O Lord, which Thou Hast Made for Thee to Dwell in, in the Sanctuary, O Lord, which Thy Hands Have Established.

The Lord Shall Reign for ever and ever. For the horse of Pharaoh went in with his chariots and with his horsemen into the sea, and The Lord Brought again the waters of the sea upon them; but the children of Israel went on dry land in the midst of the sea. And Miriam the prophetess, the sister of Aaron, took a timbrel in her hand; and all the women went out after her with timbrels and with dances. And Miriam answered them, Sing ye to The Lord, for He Hath Triumphed Gloriously; the horse and his rider hath He Thrown into the sea".

Conclusion

To The Only Wise God, I Give All Honor and Praise in The Name of Jesus Christ. I'm often Teaching The People of God this Fact, that whenever The Engrafted Words of God is being Preached and Teach, there is one clear Fact that is always experience by those who have received of that Word, and that is, that The Father Is Always In Connection with the Souls of man who have found themselves to be The Good Ground. The only reflection of a man that is still linked to The Father of The Universe is the Soul of a man, therefore when God Speaks, if the Soul of a man is furnished to be The Good Ground, then that Soul will be in a receptive mood of acknowledging that God Has Spoken.

The One God Ministry has brought forth conclusive proof to identify The God of The Universe As Being Only ONE; it would be a great consolation if all People, Nations, Languages and Dominions accept this fact, but according to History and The Revelations that only God Can Reveal, it suggest that it is always a Remnant, The

Tenth, The Tithes of Saints that are Granted the sure Approval of Receiving what God Has Revealed.

I'm joyful within my Soul that I was found worthy to put together A Golden Manuscript in this order that Reflects The Mind of God unto People, Nations, Languages and Dominions. God Using me and Being pleased with me is my sure reward. If it's only ten of this Book is sold, then I'm confident that the ten people that have bought this Book Entitled "GOD IS", it will surely manifest upon their lives that they will now become Tools for God to Use to Reveal to other People, Nations, Languages and Dominions that God Is Indeed ONE.

I Pray that every Soul that comes in contact with The Message of this Book will be forever Changed to The Purpose of God's Will Being Done.

Unto The Established Name of Jesus Christ I Give All Glory, Honor and Praise. From The Ministry of The Church of Jesus Christ Fellowship Savannah Cross, Jamaica, West Indies, God's Blessing Always, Amen.

"Thank you for inviting The Living Spirit of God within your life, it's now your job to water that which you have received to therefore become The Fruit Tree for God's Glory in The Almighty Name of Jesus Christ, Amen!"